Under the Table

Rakesh Singh

BlueRose ONE.com
Stories Matter
NewDelhi • London

BLUEROSE PUBLISHERS
India | U.K.

BlueRose ONE.com
Stories Matter
NewDelhi • London

For permissions requests or inquiries regarding this publication, please contact:

BLUEROSE PUBLISHERS
www.BlueRoseONE.com
info@bluerosepublishers.com
+91 8882 898 898
+4407342408967

ISBN: 978-93-6783-703-0

Cover design: Shubham
Typesetting: Sagar

First Edition: November 2024

About the Book

Dear Readers and Youth of India and the World,

This brief, 17-chapter book dives deep into the pressing issues of corruption and bribery that we, the common and middle-class people, face every day. It's a story of how we often sacrifice our work, our dignity, and sometimes even our dreams to navigate a world where bribery has become a tragic norm. I've poured my personal experiences into these pages, sharing how I, too, became a victim of corrupt politicians and a broken system.

The middle class constantly battles to meet even the most basic needs, living for the happiness and security of their families. In this quiet struggle, so many people sacrifice their own lives and dreams—a sacrifice only they and their souls truly understand.

Now think about it: if inflation hits its peak, how many politicians would actually feel the impact? None. Politicians live in a bubble, sheltered in mansions, served with lavish food, enjoying a lifestyle far removed from ours. Their focus? Criticizing opponents, rather than understanding the struggles we endure.

If this book manages to bring even the smallest change—if it shifts even 0.01% of society's mind-set for the better—then I will feel that I have contributed something meaningful to my country. That would bring me immense happiness, knowing I left a mark before I leave this world.

Contents

Introduction

The Scope of Corruption- Corruption-Let's Find the solution

First, we, the common people of this country, must understand what we call *corruption*. When any task—big or small—cannot proceed without a demand for money, when someone asks you for a "donation" or "fund" as a bribe, and when you feel trapped, believing there's no way out but to pay, *that* is corruption. And both the person taking the bribe and the one offering it are equally responsible for this wrongdoing. We know it's wrong, yet we treat it as an unavoidable custom. But this is not some essential tradition to be followed at all costs; it's the worst practice we have turned into an unspoken rule. The shocking part? Today, almost everyone follows this "custom" eagerly, some even finding excitement in the act. Could there be anything more disheartening?

Those willing to compromise their conscience by paying bribes are *more* responsible for this corruption. Why? Because no one wants to wait their turn anymore. Everyone believes they have the "right" to skip the line, to have their work done first. "I'm too busy to wait," they think. And this selfish mentality fuels corruption, making it a grave concern and a tragic reality.

For those who think, "What difference can my actions make?"—understand this: true change starts with a single step. Your effort alone can spark a movement. If you take that step, others will follow naturally. Don't underestimate the power of one person's courage to stand against corruption. Together, we can create a society that values honesty and integrity.

Corruption touches every corner of Indian society, from the elite halls of government to the simplest street vendor. It's the under-the-table money required to get a legal document, the expected "tip" for a service that should be free, and the invisible tax on citizens just trying to live their lives. Corruption is deeply woven into the fabric of Indian life, eroding trust, emptying wallets, and stealing the hope for a fairer, brighter future. But why has this become so entrenched? And how can we begin to uproot it?

For the common Indian, who is most often exposed to corruption at base level in their daily life, it has left a scar. Corruption is an anchor, and whether that's an unspoken bribe to fast track a passport application, a sort of informal "fee" to get your kid into a good school, or something akin to money under the table in public health care; Every citizen is impacted by it, yet its burden falls most on the average joe—the shopkeeper, the farmer, teacher, and homemaker. For some, it is a hassle and for others, this determines if they have either food on the table or go to bed with an empty stomach.

India is a land of diversity. But one thing that sadly unites us is the presence of corruption at various levels. Whether it's a small bribe to get your electricity connection fixed or a larger sum to win a contract, the system often demands more than it should. Corruption has taken root because of long-standing cultural, social, and political reasons.

Let’s look at a simple example: getting a driving license. Have you ever tried getting one without paying an agent? Most people say it's nearly impossible. The process is long, confusing, and often requires some "under-the-table" payment to speed things up. This is just one of the many day-to-day instances where corruption creeps into our lives.

Chapter 1

Understanding the Roots of Corruption

Corruption has become, inescapably, part of India's story; how did it get that way? Only by understanding the roots can we retake India.

Historical Context: Where It All Began

Corruption did not happen overnight. That outlook is as old as the nation itself, dating back to colonial days when power holders viewed the multitude as a means of production rather than human beings. Under British rule, the path to exploitation and bribery was paved for survival in a system that worked in the favour of only a handful at the top. And well after independence, this structure of inequality persisted, quietly sliding into the political contours of post-colonial India.

With democracy, came channels for corruption. Politicians offered jobs and favors for votes, businesses learned to do the bare minimum, and power needed a price tag. Gradually, it simply became part of life to bribe or be bribed; something that people learnt to live with

How Corruption Took Root in India's Bureaucracy

Picture yourself standing in a large queue at the government office, to acquire the documentation you require for a fresh business license. Hours go by, and you remain unmoved. Then someone leans towards you and like a whisper says: "I can get it for you today for the right price." This is not a sporadic narrative — it is the perennial tale of countless Indians.

India's bureaucratic system was designed for the purpose of serving the people but it has been an obstruction to Bharat as a nation. For ordinary citizens, there are unnecessary obstacles and without bribes, even simplest of things seem impossible. For many, it feels like we are ensnared in a series of hoops and hurdles, each one requiring something more to tip the scales of possibility. Which then turns a system that should be equitable into one where the highest bidder gets served.

Imagine if Gandhiji had thought, "What can one person achieve? Would I be a fool to take this step alone?" But look at what he accomplished. With unwavering determination, he drove out the British and shook an entire nation. That's why they say, "Fortune favors the brave." People flocked to him, inspired and ready to sacrifice everything because they believed in his vision.

Now ask yourself—if one person could move a nation, why can't we change a system? If a single voice can shatter mountains of oppression, surely we can break down a flawed system, a mere stone in comparison.

Action begins with thought. When your thoughts push you toward action, and when that action is aimed at justice and progress, it transforms you. You rise to stand among the great. But greatness isn't reached without effort, without resolve. Without your drive, your determination, no change can happen.

Too often, we see people passionately discussing big issues, and they lose themselves in the thrill of debate. But remember, only talking won't solve anything. Change demands action. Don't let your passion fade in mere words—let it push you forward, let it drive you to do something real.

If you only plan or think about an exam, you'll never see the results. To taste success, you have to take action—you must sit for the test to experience the fruits of your effort. Without sowing seeds, you cannot expect a harvest; without getting your hands dirty, you cannot clean the dirt. You don't have a magic wand that allows you to make things better without touching them. Involvement is necessary to solve any problem.

To stand out as an extraordinary person, distance yourself from those who waste time discussing trivial matters or aimlessly passing time. Value your hours, channel them toward a meaningful goal. I truly believe that any good deed, however small, brings happiness. It's not about the scale of the action—big or small, a good deed is always good. When you do something for others, for the welfare of society, a powerful warmth fills your heart. This is a feeling beyond words, something only you can feel within.

Someone once said, "If you want to feel important, make others feel valued." In every community, there are two types of people: those who will support you, encourage you, and stand by you when you fight for a just cause; and those who will neither support nor appreciate you, choosing instead to silently watch or even discourage you. Aim to be the first type—the one who supports, appreciates, and encourages those fighting for the common good.

It's all too common to see local leaders, councilors, or MLAs doing public work with hidden motives, aiming merely to attract attention and secure votes. If, by any chance, they find out that you support another party, they might go to lengths to make life difficult for you. Such behavior does not deserve our respect, nor can it be called "good work." True good work expects nothing in return. It doesn't rely on votes, threats, or manipulation.

Do good with clear, positive intentions, and you'll see followers and support gather naturally. Only selfless acts, done without personal gain, can truly be called good—and sometimes, even great. To this day, it's unclear why a genuine leader would need to beg for votes. When someone is honest and truly devoted to public service, the people will recognize and support them without needing empty promises or flashy schemes.

This is the 21st century. People are aware of your motives and perspectives. So be honest—show who you truly are. Remove the mask and let the people judge: Are you a divine guide, or are you a demon? Are you a true ambassador of good for us, or are you our oppressor?

People must understand the effects of corruption and how it seeps into their lives. Corruption is the root of countless evils—poverty, illiteracy, unemployment, frustration, even suicide. Just as necessity is the mother of invention, it wouldn't be wrong to say, "Corruption is the mother of destruction."

Because of corruption, poverty exists. India, our country, has been rich since ancient times, even up to the pre-British era. Today, India has enough wealth to eradicate poverty. But thousands of crores are hidden away in Swiss banks as black money. Imagine—the sum is so vast it could eliminate poverty and address many of our country's needs. Yet, no government has shown genuine interest in retrieving it. This is a glaring lack of political will. Retrieving this wealth is not an insurmountable task; it simply requires a firm agreement with the Swiss government. The money is no longer the property of corrupt politicians—it belongs to the people of India.

I don't need to prescribe the specific policies or agreements needed to bring back this wealth; our policymakers are more than capable. But I do know this: it's not an impossible task, and our government has the power to accomplish it if only they would show the will to act.

Let me show you how illiteracy and poverty are interconnected, each feeding into the other. When families struggle to afford even necessities, how can they possibly bear the expense of educating their children? The government may have launched several schemes for free, compulsory education for children under 14, but in reality, very few schools follow this mandate. Under the Integrated Child Development Scheme (ICDS), schools are supposed to provide free mid-day meals to children. But the sad truth is that, from top to bottom, school staff loot the funds allocated for these meals, exploiting the system in the name of the scheme. They know no one will come to check the quality of the ingredients used in these meals. There should be regular, unannounced inspections by the Food Corporation of India in every school to ensure that these children receive what they deserve.

Take, for example, the horrific mid-day meal tragedy that shocked India on July 16, 2013, in Bihar's Chhapra district. Twenty-three children, aged between 5 and 10, died after consuming food at the Dharmashati Gandaman Primary School (classes I to V) in

Saran district, 90 km northwest of Patna. Investigations revealed that the container used to store the edible oil was contaminated with pesticides. The negligence that led to this tragedy is nothing short of a national disgrace.

After this incident, the government imposed strict guidelines to ensure the safe execution of the mid-day meal scheme. First, school heads were required to taste the food before serving it to children. Second, only ISI-certified oil could be used for cooking. Third, all food had to be stored in covered utensils. Fourth, kitchens, storage areas, and utensils had to be kept clean. Fifth, teachers had to ensure that students washed their hands before eating. And lastly, daily checks by new inspection teams were mandated.

But let's face it—this is just one example. For every story like this, there are thousands, perhaps even millions, of similar tragedies across the country.

But the problems remain the same. Creating policies or making announcements alone isn't enough—what truly matters is their implementation. Who is ensuring that these measures are actually followed? Who will make sure that school heads taste the food before serving it to students, or that kitchens, storage, and utensils are kept clean and sanitary? If schools receive advance notice of an inspection, nothing will change—they simply prepare a perfect scene to pass inspection. Regular and unannounced inspections are essential to catch issues and reveal the truth.

Because of systemic issues like corruption, poverty, and illiteracy, India still holds the label of a "developing country." The gap between developing and developed nations is so vast that closing it seems almost like a distant dream—a dream hindered by a long bridge filled with obstacles, built by corruption, poverty, and illiteracy. Our politicians and the system show no will to cross this bridge, and without that crossing, true development remains out of reach.

Even more troubling, the political system often turns a deaf ear to anyone who dares to expose these issues, whether it's a lone individual or a larger group seeking justice. Instead of addressing the matter, they criticize those speaking out, and they'll go to great lengths to silence them. If the person persists with determination, the government uses its last resort: throwing them behind bars. After that, their strong voice is silenced, their determination crushed. And this happens largely due to a lack of strong, unwavering support.

We need to understand the difference between mere support and *strong* support. Support isn't about numbers; it's about courage. Often, people measure support by the crowd size. But what good is a large crowd if it runs the moment circumstances turn unfavourable ? Strong supporters are different. Suppose you have the support of a hundred people, but when the police start wielding their batons, sixty of them flee. It's the remaining forty who are your true supporters—people who will stand by you to the last breath, no matter the situation.

If someone isn't capable of leading the charge, then be a strong supporter. Stand beside those fighting for a good cause, for the welfare of society. You'll emerge as a pillar of strength, known for your determination. Instead of being a silent spectator, join the movement. Become part of the change. A man can't reach the sky without trying to fly. In the same way, if you don't take a stand, you can't be part of meaningful change. Know that the road will be long and the goal hard to achieve. You may face injuries and setbacks, but let those be physical wounds, not mental defeats. A physically hurt person can still reach their goal if their mind stays strong. But a mentally broken person cannot.

Victory requires a steady mind, ready to face challenges. Prepare yourself, focus on your goal, and stay true to it—no matter what comes your way.

Imagine yourself as a student, and your board exam center is far from your town, city, or village. What do you feel? You won't waste time worrying about the condition of the roads, how many potholes there might be, or how many bumps you'll endure along the way. When it comes to achieving your dreams, these things won't matter. If you're truly determined to pass your exam and reach your goals, you'll go—no matter what. Similarly, anyone with a deep desire to serve their country will do so without hesitation, regardless of circumstances.

Remember, the path of truth and integrity has never been easy. Truth takes time to triumph, but it always prevails. There's no shortcut on this road; it's a test of patience and resilience. The path of deceit, however, is tempting, easy, and littered with shortcuts. It's alluring because it promises instant rewards—quick money, easy gains. But that path is deceptive, leading not to lasting success but to ruin. A single shortcut can turn a life into a living hell. The rapid rise up the ladder may feel thrilling, but when the illusion shatters, you're left plummeting even faster than you rose. You'll fall from the height of pride, money, and reputation just as quickly as you gained them—if not faster.

So, my friend, never consider shortcuts in life, especially those that compromise your character. What's the point of success if it comes at the cost of your peace, dignity, and chance to stand strong when you fall? In life, there are always two choices: the right one and the wrong one. Too often, people choose the wrong because it seems like an easier way to get ahead. They think it's the fast lane to wealth, without the struggle of honest work. But this path offers only hollow titles, fake pride, and dignity devoid of humanity. At best, it brings a lifetime of shame and regret, a life devoid of true joy.

Illegal practices may seem pleasurable in the moment, but there's no real joy in them. They rob you of everything worthwhile. It's like searching for a treasure, only to realize it's empty—a fruit with no sweetness, a flower with no fragrance. Anyone who believes otherwise is setting themselves up for ruin. They're choosing a life of imprisonment, if not death.

True determination cannot be shaken by a passing storm of greed. If it wavers, then it was never truly determination. Determination is the foundation of your life. If it's strong, you can build upon it and reach incredible heights without fear of collapse. Use it wisely and in a positive direction. If you build your life on dishonesty, remember: it will be demolished one day. A life built on deceit is destined to crumble.

People who enjoy illegal practices, living only in the present and not caring about the future, often find themselves in trouble later on, seeking help when it's too late. But by then, no one comes to their aid. For example, if a person chooses the wrong way to earn money, thinking it will make their life better, they often fail to realize the dire consequences. It only takes a few seconds for their life to go from heaven to hell.

It deeply saddens me to think that some of our corrupt politicians have changed the meaning of India. I want to ask them: What does

India stand for? As far as I know, I want to ask the government: Is this the true meaning of India? Does it stand for:

I – Is
N-Nation
D – Demand
I – Innocent
A – Arrest

Because if the answer is "no," then why is it that anyone who dares to raise their voice against any wrongdoing is sent behind bars? Their voice is crushed, silenced. We have a great example in the India Against Corruption movement. Let me remind you, and take you back to that time when the whole country witnessed the back-to-back arrests of Baba Ramdev and anti-corruption crusader Anna Hazare. They were protesting against corruption, demanding that black money be brought back to our country, and that those responsible be punished by the law. There was no harm in their demands, and they weren't protesting against the national interest. They only wanted what was rightfully ours.

As far as national interest is concerned, let me tell you: your "interest" is no longer interest if it is not aligned with the welfare of the country. If you have not shown an interest that benefits the nation, then what is the use of it? We all know the action the government took against these brave voices. The government created this situation for itself. So, it would not be wrong to say that the government follows the principle of "eat and let others eat." Here, "others" refers to their ministers and allies. They assured them with a simple, yet chilling sentence: "Nothing to worry, sir." Why? Because they wield a power called the Brahmastra.

We all have seen this character in mythological serials like Ramayana and Mahabharata — when a situation gets out of control, or when things turn against them, they have to use their last weapon, the Brahmastra, to defeat the enemy and regain control. Similarly, the government, when the protests got out of hand or started turning against them, used their last weapon, the police force — the Brahmastra — to disperse the crowd and take full control. Ultimately, the innocent but brave people had to surrender because, as the people of India, we believe in peaceful protests. We cannot allow ourselves to become rage-fueled or violent, even in the face of overwhelming force.

Take another example: the whistleblower. A whistleblower is someone who raises their voice against any wrongdoing within their institution, someone who exposes the secrets of their organization and brings the truth to light. But often, they face threats — sometimes even death threats — from their superiors for speaking out.

Edward Snowden, a contractual agent long back ago working with the National Investigation Agency of America, revealed the shocking truth that the U.S. government was conducting surveillance on all major institutions across the globe. In response, he received threats from the U.S., and even faced espionage charges framed against him. This is a familiar pattern: whenever someone dares to speak out against wrongdoing, they often find themselves boycotted by the government and even ostracized from their own society.

One can observe that when a person is about to commit a crime, or is engaged in actions that will harm their future, their mind is filled with fear—fear of what will happen if they are exposed. The person who knowingly chooses the wrong path, fully aware of the dangers ahead, will inevitably stumble, unable to take even a single step forward with confidence. On the other hand, the one who chooses the right path—knowing it is the right path to follow—walks without fear. They understand that there are no traps ahead, no pitfalls to fall into, and though the journey may be long, they will reach their destination safely.

In our country, it's like a series of bomb blasts, but this time, it's a series of scams—one after another. The Commonwealth Games scam, the 2G Spectrum scam (worth 1.76 lakh crores), the Coalgate scam, which dwarfs even the 2G scam, and the Railway scam, also known as the Uncle-Nephew-Chacha Bhatija scam (involving then-Railway Minister Pawan Kumar Bansal and his nephew). It's deeply unfortunate that while other countries are setting world records in sports, advancing in economic growth, and working to improve the lives of their citizens, we are busy setting a record in corruption—one so deep and pervasive, it may never be broken.

We are too busy, but not with the country's welfare. We are not concerned with shaping the future of our nation. We have no time to even consider what the future holds if we continue to focus only on criticizing one another.

While other nations are thinking of how to build better infrastructure, we are thinking of ways to dig into our own, ensuring it disappears, leaving only the hollowed-out structure behind. While others dream of reaching the moon, we dream only of the silver spoon—believing that if we make enough money during our lifetimes, our next generation will inherit a silver spoon in their mouths.

Concerning our country's present situation here is a poem that I composed and would like to present before you.

Corruption, corruption, corruption! Everyone is shouting about corruption,
But no one has time to even think about its solution."

"To take part in the race of personal selection,
Our leaders are busy, only when it comes to election."

"To fight any election, One does not require any qualification,
But one must have a 'Dabangg' character with criminal connections"

"In people's representative act when supreme court makes AMENDMENT,
The government starts wondering how they can be dependent ."

"Our country is known for its secularism,
But please, stop using it as a weapon for terrorism."

"Our leaders are busy criticizing each other,
Leaving the country to depend on its real father."

In the first stanza, it speaks to what the people of India are thinking. Everyone is eager to talk about corruption, yet no one takes the time to think about the solutions, or how we can contribute to building a brighter future for our country. We all know the truth: our leaders only show up when it's time for elections. To secure our votes, they won't hesitate to come to our doorsteps, trying to prove they're the best candidate for us. But once the election is over, they forget all about us. They become busy with their power and their personal gains, and the promises they made to the people fade away.

In the second stanza, we reflect on the current state of our nation's political system. To fight an election, one doesn't need any qualifications, but the truth is, a person must have a strong, "dabang" character and criminal connections. Political parties are more than willing to give tickets to candidates who have pending criminal cases. Even knowing this, they align themselves with such individuals, going to great lengths to bring them into their parties. And the shocking fact is that these candidates win elections! But once they win, they enjoy the power they've gained, and the promises they made to the people are left unfulfilled. The changes we all hope for never come. Then, we start criticizing them, but the reality is, we're the ones who made the mistake in the first place. We, the people, only know how to regret after making mistakes. We never stop to ask: Can anyone truly win without our support? Was the candidate I voted for really the right choice? Before we vote, we must ask ourselves these hard questions. Only then can we avoid the cycle of disappointment.

Recently, when the honorable Supreme Court made an amendment to the People's Representatives Act, barring any minister found guilty and convicted by a court from contesting elections for ten years, it created a ripple of change. Lalu Prasad Yadav, the former Chief Minister of Bihar, became the first prominent example of this act after he was convicted in the multi-crore fodder scam and sentenced to five years in jail. Now, he cannot contest any election for at least ten years. The Supreme Court's amendment created the first opportunity to hold corrupt leaders accountable. But instead of welcoming this amendment, the government, which should have praised it, called it "gruesome."

Instead of appreciating it, they became irritated. This is the irony of our political system. Power-hungry politicians will do anything to hold onto their seats and remain in control, no matter how many corrupt actions they have to conceal. The ruling parties now fear the consequences of losing their grip, and we, the people, are left to pick up the pieces.

In the third and final stanza, we look at the nature of our leaders and the future of our country. India is known worldwide for its secularism, where all religions are respected equally, without distinction of caste or creed. But sadly, some leaders exploit this. They thrust themselves into the race for credit, attempting to be seen as the "godfather" of one religion or another, claiming they are the only ones capable of stopping communal violence and bringing harmony. They say, "Vote for me, and I will change your future," all the while blowing their own trumpets. These leaders want to secure as many votes as possible. Whenever there is a riot or communal unrest, they rush to the scene, not to resolve the issue, but to position themselves as saviors, offering nothing more than a few words. They never focus on the true welfare of the people or the country. Instead, they are busy criticizing each other while leaving the nation to rely on its true Father—the almighty God, the Creator of the universe. If our leaders stopped fighting each other and worked together, then something meaningful could happen. They could create a future where the welfare of the people is the true priority.

In 2012, we bought a house in Kharagpur, West Bengal, my birthplace, where my childhood memories and friends are still part of my life. One day, I went to the ward councilor's office to get a signature on the municipality mutation form. As soon as she learned that we had bought a new house in her locality, she asked for money as a "donation" to her party. This is a common practice in many parts of West Bengal—whenever someone buys a new house, they are expected to give 2% of the property value as a donation. If you refuse, you won't be safe, and your documentation work will remain stuck.

When I was asked for 2% of the property value, I was shocked. This was the first time I had encountered such a situation. Before that, I had only heard about bribes being asked in the name of donations. I went home and told my parents and my elder brother the whole story. After discussing it, I went back to the local ward councilor's office, requesting her to sign the form for municipal mutation and the water connection. She repeated the same demand for a donation.

I was helpless, but I explained that 2% of the property value was too much for us. We were from a lower-middle-class family, and my father had just retired. My father worked for the Railway Protection Force (RPF) and retired as a head constable in January 2012. Since he was the head constable, his pension wasn't enough to buy a house. So, my elder brother, who worked in Gurugram, took out a loan to help buy the house. My father and brother pooled their resources for this dream.

I didn't share this story to seek sympathy, but because it was the truth. I wanted the councilor to understand the reality of people like us—those from lower-middle-class families who have to take out loans for 20-30 years to buy a house. My father had spent his entire life working hard, waiting for his retirement to finally provide a home for his family. And yet, a person sitting in a comfortable office, with all the amenities, demands lakhs of rupees without lifting a finger.

It made me think for a moment: people like her live such a different life. They seem blessed, while people like my father, who worked tirelessly for his family, had to wait for retirement to fulfill his dream. My father spent half of his life living in a small government quarter with a single room, while people like the councilor get lakhs in a second, without doing anything to deserve it. This, I thought, is what they call life.

Since my father worked for the South Eastern Railway, his job was transferable. Every 2-3 years, he would be transferred to a new location. To ensure we didn't suffer from constant transfers, he kept us in Kharagpur, where I was born. He would visit us once a month, staying only 1-2 days at a time. In total, he spent just 8 years with his family. He passed away in May 2021 during the second wave of COVID-19.

Finally, after bargaining and multiple requests, the counselor showed some mercy and gave me a discount. However, I had to give money in the name of a "donation" to the party. In reality, I was asked to give a bribe, and I felt helpless, so I handed over the money just to get my paperwork done. Once the mutation was completed in my name, I had to apply to transfer the electricity bill as well. But all these tasks had been pending until I paid the bribe.

This practice of paying money under the guise of anything is not limited to Kharagpur; it's everywhere. Let me share another experience. One day, I went to the Regional Transport Office (RTO) to get my four-wheeler driving license. After applying online and booking an appointment, I took all my original documents with me to the office. Despite having everything in hand, I was asked to submit multiple documents. If you missed even one document, you'd have to book another appointment and revisit the office.

On the other hand, I saw people who came through brokers. They didn't have to wait in long queues, didn't need to submit documents personally, and had all their paperwork handled by the broker. They were given direct entry for the online test.

What does this show? It shows that bribery makes life easier and hassle-free, doesn't it? You skip the queue, bypass the documentation process, and save your precious time. But those who either don't have the money for a bribe or refuse to give one face immense struggles. They stand in long queues, endure repeated visits, and in the end, they are left with nothing but frustration. So, whose life is truly better? I want you to reflect on this as you lie down tonight.

Honestly speaking, it's not the fault of the person who gives the bribe; it's the corrupt system that forces people into corruption. Sometimes, a person feels helpless in the face of this system and gives in, just to get their work done. But if work were done without harassing anyone, bribes would cease to exist.

Everyday Corruption – A Way of Life?

1. **The Cost of a Birth Certificate**: Describe the hoops parents often jump through just to get a birth certificate for their child. They might face delays, indifferent clerks, and ultimately, demands for a "facilitation fee." Such fees, though unofficial, have become expected to "smoothen the process." Explain how this not only burdens parents financially but also dehumanizes a basic right.

2. **Education System – Paying for Grades**: Acknowledge the pressure students and parents face to get admission to prestigious schools or colleges. Show

how bribes or “donations” are often required to secure a seat, even if a student is fully qualified. Talk about how students lose faith in the fairness of the system and how it fosters distrust in institutions meant to nurture their futures.

3. **Healthcare – When Bribes Decide Lives**: Illustrate a scenario in which a family needs urgent medical care but is delayed because an official asks for money to prioritize their case. Describe the impact of these situations on a family’s trust in public services and the sense of helplessness when health—something so crucial—is affected by corruption.

Police Encounters – The Price of Protection

Many experience encounters where even simple requests—like filing a report—come with implicit money expectations. Show how the police force, which should protect citizens, can often seem out of reach unless bribes are paid. Include an anecdote or two where citizens are forced to “pay up” to avoid false charges or gain justice

Chapter 2

The Impact of Corruption on Daily Life

The Cost of Corruption in Everyday Life

Corruption does not only rob money, it robs hope, honour and opportunities. For instance, a mother is attempting to get her child admitted into a reputable school. She may have the merit and the ambition, but there is still an implication that a "donation" will be required to get a place. If another reason not to leave an abusive relationship; the money comes in handy, but when you can't pay your child misses out on a good education and a better life.

In healthcare, it is more tragic. This has caused certain patients to cough up extra for emergency services or treatments. Visualize if you need to decide on saving the life of a beloved one for whom bribes might be able to help if your budget could not. Not only their hard earned money, which is expensive for an ordinary citizen, but also hopes that humanity and fairness still exist.

The Emotional and Financial Toll on Families

Far beyond the money lost, corruption steals our peace of mind. Unfortunately, it creates frustration, helplessness and above all anger. For a labouring dad who has to cough up a bribe just to stay in work or for his children to be treated decently, the injustice is hard to swallow. Corruption transforms ordinary people's hard-earned money into "hidden costs," bleeding families dry and destroying aspirations.

Kids notice their parents who aren't making money, and they get introduced early to the fact that life isn't always fair with class structure. They have been raised in an environment where a little under-the-table exchange will more likely land them on their feet and least find its way to making a donation, hence integrity can be perceived as an impediment. Such degenerating values starts taking root in society, distorting one's moral compass and giving birth to demons in every human heart.

Once upon a time, about ten years ago, 1 USD was equal to 45-50 INR. Now, its value has almost doubled. The current exchange rate is around 84 INR for 1 USD. In just a few years, the value of the dollar has surged, while our rupee continues to lose its strength every single day, every single year. The government explains this as a result of fiscal and current account deficits.

In simple terms, the current account deficit occurs when the value of our imports—whether goods, services, or investment income—is greater than the value of our exports. This means we are buying more from the world than we are selling, and the rupee weakens because of it.

A fiscal deficit, on the other hand, happens when the government's expenditure exceeds its revenue in a given year. When we use these economic terms to justify the weakening of the Indian rupee, we should realize that if things continue this way, we might soon see the rupee cross the century mark against the dollar.

But it doesn't have to be this way.

We feel the sting of this loss. Every time we try to buy something from abroad, we are reminded of our dwindling power in the global market.

But why should we accept this fate? Why should we sit back and watch as our country's wealth is drained away? Why should we let the government's economic mismanagement and the global powers play games with our lives?

The truth is, we don't have to. We can fight back. We can demand accountability, not just from our leaders, but from ourselves. We can begin by understanding the forces that shape our economy, by questioning the systems that allow this injustice to thrive, and by holding those responsible to account. It's time we stop letting ourselves be passive victims of economic policies that only serve the rich and powerful.

This is about more than just numbers and statistics. This is about our future. This is about our children's future. If we let the rupee continue to weaken, if we let the current account and fiscal deficits continue to grow, we risk losing not just our currency, but our very dignity as a nation.

It's time for change. It's time to rise up and demand better. It's time to take control of our economy, our resources, and our future.

• Indian Currency and Its Depreciation

With regards to Currency depreciation I would like to describe it by poem written by me for my people of the country.

'We people don't understand fiscal DEFICIT and current account DEFICIT

We only understand you ministers, only making PROFIT after PROFIT"

" Don't dig our country, your motherland anymore"

Save it or leave it, don't experiment with it for making crore"

" Save the rupees save the COUNTRY

Please stop this to make it CENTURY"

"Oh my dear Indian CURRENCY

Govt. is sleeping in hours of EMERGENCY"

"Oh my dear rupee you were not like THAT

This is our corrupt system that makes you FLAT"

"Fall in rupee, government termed it so-called DEPRECIATION

At the same time they want from us an APPRECIATION"

"Soon there will be an end of your fighting HOUR

Once people in India awake, you will gain power

Stanza 1

"We people don't understand fiscal DEFICIT and current account DEFICIT We only understand you ministers, only making PROFIT and PROFIT"

As the poet, I'm speaking directly to the readers, expressing a sentiment shared by many ordinary citizens. We don't grasp the complex economic terms like fiscal deficit and current account deficit. What we do understand is how our leaders and ministers seem to be focused solely on making profit for themselves. This stanza captures the frustration of the common man with the political elite, highlighting a disconnect between the government's economic jargon and the lived reality of the people.

Stanza 2

"Don't dig our country, your motherland anymore Save it or leave it, don't experiment with it for making crore"

Here, I'm pleading with the leaders to stop exploiting our beloved country. I urge them to either save our nation or step aside if they can't do so. The phrase "don't experiment with it for making crore" conveys the anger towards those who treat the country as a playground for their financial gains. This stanza is a call to action, urging the ministers to act responsibly and ethically.

Stanza 3

"Save the rupees save the COUNTRY Please stop this to make it CENTURY"

In this stanza, I'm emphasizing the importance of preserving the value of our currency. The fate of our country is tied to the strength of the rupee, and I plead for immediate action to halt the policies that are devaluing it. The goal is to ensure a prosperous future, spanning a century, by taking decisive steps now.

Stanza 4

"Oh my dear Indian CURRENCY Govt. is sleeping in hours of EMERGENCY"

Here, I personify the Indian currency, expressing a deep concern for its wellbeing. I lament that while the currency suffers, the government remains inactive during this critical period. This stanza conveys a sense of urgency and disappointment in the government's lack of response to the economic crisis.

Stanza 5

"Oh my dear rupee you were not like THAT This is our corrupt system that makes you FLAT"

Reflecting on the past, I remember a time when the rupee was strong and stable. I point to systemic corruption as the culprit behind its decline. This stanza nostalgically recalls better days while condemning the corruption that has led to the rupee's downfall.

Stanza 6

"Fall in rupee, government termed it so-called DEPRECIATION At the same time they want from us an APPRECIATION"

In this stanza, I highlight the hypocrisy of the government. They label the fall in the rupee as "depreciation" while simultaneously demanding gratitude and appreciation from the citizens. This stark contrast underscores the government's insensitivity and disconnect from the people's struggles.

Stanza 7

"Soon there will be an end of your fighting HOUR Once people in India awake, you will gain power"

I end on a hopeful note, predicting a time when the people of India will awaken and take charge. When this happens, the rupee will regain its strength and value. This final stanza is a call for collective action and empowerment, suggesting that the ultimate power lies in the hands of the awakened populace.

Chapter 3

Bribery and the Election Game

How Bribes Shape Democracy in India

No one says, in a Democracy, every vote should carry weight. Yet elections are a buyer-seller market in India where you buy loyalty and sell yourself. Politicians make promises with one hand and move the money with the other, and the people get nothing. For lots of poor individuals, a single money carrot or allotment of basic provisions can easily resemble an avenue. But this is a temporary advantage that attaches them for the foreseeable future to leaders who may have no intention of serving their interests at all.

No wonder folks get frustrated voting for change only to find they have just installed a new jockey on the same broken horse. Election after election, democracy wears its final magin while bribery and backdoor deals decide the game of power.

The Price of Bribery

Bribery seems like a quick fix. But in the long run, it costs us far more. Every bribe paid sets a precedent for the next one. Over time, it creates a system where people without the ability to pay suffer the most. The rich and powerful get their way, while the common man is left struggling.

Take, for example, a farmer in rural India who needs a loan to buy seeds. He is asked to pay a small bribe to speed up the process. If he doesn't pay, his application will gather dust. If he pays, he is left with less money to invest in his crops. It's a vicious cycle that affects not just one family but entire communities.

1. **The Election Game**: Discuss how money flows during elections and the quid pro quo expected by those funding campaigns. Use examples of recent political scandals in India where election spending is not transparent, and funds are misused, affecting democratic fairness. Explain how candidates focus on securing seats rather than addressing the needs of the people.

2. **Policy Manipulation – Who Benefits?**: Provide an example of policies that appear beneficial on the surface but have loopholes intentionally included for the benefit of certain corporations or individuals. Show how the political elite creates laws that prioritize the interests of a few wealthy groups over the broader public, especially those already struggling.

3. **Public Projects – Where the Money Really Goes**: Outline a situation involving a public infrastructure project, like building a road or school. Walk readers through how inflated budgets and kickbacks lead to poorly constructed facilities that decay quickly, leaving communities to suffer while the funds intended for them are siphoned away.

The Silent Victims

Corruption and bribery hit the poorest and most vulnerable the hardest. The common man pays twice—once in money and again in missed opportunities. A simple medical check-up in a government hospital often requires extra "fees" to get quicker service. It's not uncommon to hear stories of families paying to get a hospital bed or even basic treatment.

In urban areas, getting a house registered in your name, obtaining a water connection, or enrolling your child in a good school often comes with an added "cost." For those who can't afford to pay these bribes, the system works against them.

Chapter 4

The Economic Impact of Corruption

How Corruption Stalls Economic Growth

Corruption is, to all intents and purposes, a cancer whose fingers are deeply entrenched and spreading in the Indian sub-continent. The investments returned could benefit greatly the economy, however private individuals prefer to hoard them. The resources intended for people's needs are, many times, nowhere to be found. Roads rot before they are built, supplies are non-existent in schools, hospitals accommodate more patients than there are doctors. Every plan that has been chartered to make the community better ends up blown with modesty from all their priorities because of the people in charge.

In the case of small business owners, corruption is in every sense of the word, a cumulative effect. The local shop keeper for instance might be forced to pay local corrupt officials bribes in order to keep his shop running, therefore increasing the overheads such that fair competition becomes a far-fetched objective. Because of the unfair competition, innovation becomes a non-starter and growth is but a pipe dream for the common enterpriser.

Chapter 5

Real-Life Stories of Courage Against Corruption

Individuals Who Took a Stand

Despite the prevalence of corruption, some individuals are willing to speak out against the rot and instead stand for integrity. These are people who will not succumb to the system, who will ask for accountability and will seek justice. There's the tale of a young civil servant who dared to give evidence of financial misspending in her department, and thereby, jeopardised her career in the process of bringing attention to the wastage of public resources. There's the story of a teacher who, rather than demanding a bribe for awarding good grades, decided to instil in her students that they should work hard for the scores. Jeopardized

These people are indeed a reminder to the rest of us that the fact that corruption has taken deep roots in our society does not mean that there are no courageous men and women. Their experiences are able to motivate other people to rise and question the existing order, and dream of a world they can aspire to where there are no kickbacks and shady practices. They demonstrate to us that change is possible if one person decides it is more convenient to be honest than to take the easy way out.

Real-Life Stories of Bravery

Despite the overwhelming presence of corruption, there are people who stand up against it. One such story is of a schoolteacher in Rajasthan who refused to pay a bribe to get his rightful pension. His fight lasted years, but he finally won in court. Another is a group of women in Maharashtra who, after years of exploitation by corrupt officials, formed a self-help group to fight back.

These stories inspire us to believe that change is possible, even when the system feels stacked against us.

Politics and Corruption

Politics and corruption are often two sides of the same coin in India. From election campaigns to policy-making, money speaks louder than words. Political leaders often make tall promises, but the money that flows behind the scenes controls which promises get fulfilled. Funds meant for public welfare projects sometimes vanish, lining the pockets of a few.

Take the example of road construction in a small town. The government allots a significant budget, but what you see is a poorly built road that needs repairs within months. Why? Because the money meant for good materials and proper work went into someone's pocket. The public pays taxes but gets substandard services in return.

Chapter 6

The Way Forward for India

Empowering Citizens and Building Transparency

As long as citizens are empowered, that is when there is a brighter chance for a corruption-free India. Change begins when people know their rights and have mechanisms through which they can make officials answerable. Technology has the potential to be revolutionary. People can submit complaints about corruption through their phones and there are databases that enhance transparency and social media has its own functions to promote people's voices. When there is a common voice for honesty among people, the average positive response can start to shift.

For the youth, one key aspect is education. Teaching children about the critical role of honesty, justice and fairness will ensure children grow to be adults who focus on mass ethics instead of quick selfish profits. Such children will denounce bribery and misuse of power as they develop and will expect a better society when they are adults.

The Way Forward: A Hope for Tomorrow

India is at a crossroads. With the rise of digital governance and a growing awareness of citizens' rights, there's hope that corruption can be reduced. E-governance initiatives like Aadhaar-linked services and direct benefit transfers (DBT) are slowly cutting out middlemen. Transparency in public dealings is increasing, and many people are beginning to speak up.

But this battle cannot be won by the government alone. Every Indian citizen has a role to play. We must demand accountability, report corruption, and refuse to participate in the cycle of bribery. Together, we can create a system that works for everyone

Chapter 7

Social and Cultural Impact of Corruption

Trust in Institutions: A Broken Relationship

If in society's governance structures corruption exists, then no faith can be placed in the institutions. More often than not, when a society begins to perceive their leaders, their judges, police officers and teachers as "out to get them," a concerning level of cynicism arises. This barbaric mistrust tends to develop in a similar manner to a virus where if unchecked, it will erode societal structure, and take its toll on interpersonal relationships.

To a majority of people, losing trust in the public institutions puts them in an isolated and helpless position. What would it feel like, witnessing people sworn to one's protection and safety as instead exploiting the very 'victims' of the situation? That is a profound violation, and with every scandal, every law that goes unaddressed, comes unaddressed a deep feeling of this betrayal. It's one of the toughest things facing India, attempting to restore that level of confidence, yet without that confidence sustained change seems unattainable.

Loss of Moral Values in Society

When corruption becomes the norm, society's values shift subtly but dangerously. What was once considered wrong or unethical starts becoming "just the way things are." Kids who see their parents bribing officials to get basic services grow up believing that bending the rules is acceptable. A kind of moral numbness sets in, where integrity feels like an old-fashioned ideal rather than a practical way to live.

This cultural shift isn't just an abstract idea—it affects everyday interactions and relationships. As values erode, so does the fabric of society itself. If people don't feel accountable to one another, if they don't respect shared principles, it's difficult to build the unity that any community or nation needs to thrive. India's greatest strength has always been its values, its commitment to justice, honor, and unity. Reclaiming these values in the face of corruption is critical to India's future.

Everyday Corruption: What We Can Do

As ordinary citizens, we feel helpless in the face of corruption. But change begins with awareness. Saying "no" to bribes, speaking up when you see corruption, and using technology to hold people accountable are small but significant steps.

For example, digital platforms like the "MyGov" app allow citizens to report corruption. Many local communities have also started using social media to expose corrupt practices. While these actions may seem small, they create ripples that can lead to larger change.

1. **Community Resistance – The Power of Collective Action**: Describe cases where communities stood against corruption, such as refusing to pay bribes or raising awareness about corruption in their area. Show how collective action can be effective in pushing back and how communities can support each other to resist exploitation.
2. **The Role of Media and Technology**: Discuss how digital tools, such as mobile apps, social media, and citizen journalism, are helping to expose corruption. Show examples of recent scandals that came to light due to whistleblowers or online activists and how ordinary citizens are beginning to hold the powerful accountable.
3. **Reforming the System – What Needs to Change?**: Conclude with realistic steps toward reform, from increased transparency in political funding to reforms in public services. Offer hope and actionable insights for readers—helping them understand how they can contribute to change, even in small ways.

Example Section: Here's an example section you could expand to reflect the writing style and approach:

"A Seat in School – The Price We Pay"

Shalini's daughter, Priya, was a bright student. She had dreamed of studying at one of the top schools in the city. Shalini was determined to make that happen. But when she visited the school, she was shocked. "A donation of one lakh rupees," the administrator told her casually, as if it were just the cost of admission.

Shalini was taken aback. "But my daughter has scored high marks! Isn't that enough?" The administrator smiled, almost sympathetically. "It's not just about marks, madam. This is how things work."

Leaving the office, Shalini felt her dreams—and her daughter's—slipping away. She knew the system was corrupt, but until that day, she hadn't realized how deeply it would impact her own family.

In this single incident, we see a common struggle. Education, which should be a right, has been turned into a business, where merit and ambition come second to money.

By using powerful, relatable examples like these, along with a narrative style that speaks directly to readers' experiences, the book will resonate strongly with an audience frustrated by corruption. From here, we could go deeper into individual sections or examples, making sure each chapter is engaging and motivating while staying grounded in real-life scenarios and potential solutions.

Chapter 8

Bribery in the Corporate World

The Corporate-Government Nexus

The partnership between big business and government in India often serves both parties—at the expense of the common citizen. Corporations, seeking to maximize profits, find ways to influence government policies, secure favourable contracts, and avoid regulations through bribes. This corporate-government nexus creates an environment where the wealthy have the power to shape laws, often side-lining the needs of the ordinary citizen.

Imagine a corporation gaining access to natural resources or agricultural land that rightfully belongs to the people. A few powerful individuals profit, while entire communities are uprooted and left without resources. The laws meant to protect the people become tools manipulated for profit. This environment fuels frustration and resentment, as the common man realizes that money often speaks louder than justice.

Scandals That Shook the Nation

Recently, several high-profile corruption scandals have rocked India, exposing how far-reaching and damaging the issue can be. Take the example of the infamous coal allocation scam or the 2G spectrum scandal—both unveiled the deep-seated rot within major sectors of the economy. These scandals remind citizens that behind every unjust law or policy, powerful interests are often pulling the strings.

For the public, each scandal adds to the sense that corruption is inescapable. And yet, these scandals also stir something else: anger, a desire for accountability, and a demand for justice. Exposing these scandals sheds light on how deep corruption runs and highlights the importance of transparency in government and business.

Chapter 9

The Role of Education in Fighting Corruption

Teaching Integrity from a Young Age

The real fight against corruption starts with education. By teaching children about honesty, fairness, and justice, we can nurture a generation that values integrity over personal gain. Schools play a crucial role in shaping these ideals, reinforcing the notion that success achieved dishonestly is no success at all.

Imagine a classroom where students learn about ethics as passionately as they learn math or science. Imagine children who grow up understanding that every bribe paid weakens the nation they love. Education rooted in values equips young people to question corrupt practices, to hold leaders accountable, and to build a society where principles matter more than profit.

Empowering Youth Through Awareness and Activism

In today's digital age, young Indians have powerful tools at their fingertips. Social media, forums, and community platforms allow them to spread awareness, report corruption, and mobilize movements. Youth activism has already shown its potential in India, with young people stepping forward to demand changes, to hold leaders accountable, and to inspire others to do the same.

This collective energy and passion can fuel a new era of integrity and transparency in India. When young people come together, they become a formidable force—one that can challenge the norms of corruption and transform society from the ground up. Their voices, empowered by education and technology, are India's greatest hope for change

Conclusion: The Power of One

Corruption and bribery are not unstoppable forces. They thrive in silence and secrecy. The moment we decide to speak up, to say "no," to take a stand, we begin to break their hold on us. Each one of us has the power to contribute to a cleaner, fairer India. The journey will not be easy, but with every small step, we move closer to a future where honesty and hard work are rewarded, and the chains of corruption are broken

Chapter 10

Legal Framework and Anti-Corruption Measures

India's Anti-Corruption Laws and Agencies

India has several anti-corruption laws and agencies designed to fight corruption, such as the Central Bureau of Investigation (CBI), the Lokpal, and the Anti-Corruption Bureau. These institutions have been set up to investigate and prosecute cases of bribery, fraud, and other corrupt practices. In theory, these agencies serve as watchdogs, helping to maintain accountability across public and private sectors.

However, while the legal framework is in place, enforcement often falls short. The people tasked with holding the corrupt accountable are often under-resourced or influenced by political interests, which can lead to selective justice or, worse, impunity for those with power. Strengthening these agencies and freeing them from political influence is key to establishing true accountability..

Shortcomings of Existing Laws

Laws against corruption are only as effective as their implementation. In many cases, loopholes allow corrupt officials to escape punishment, and the legal process itself can be so lengthy that justice feels out of reach for the victims. Take, for example, the Prevention of Corruption Act—though intended to curb corruption, its enforcement often faces delays, and those accused can sometimes evade prosecution by using connections or bribes.

This gap between law and justice is where change is most urgently needed. When laws work in favor of the powerful, the common person feels betrayed, leading to a sense of hopelessness. Making sure laws are enforced equally and quickly is a crucial step in restoring faith in India's justice system.

Afterword: Tools for Change

In this final section, I provide practical steps and resources for fighting corruption. From online platforms where you can report corrupt activities to organizations that offer legal aid, there are ways to make a difference. Remember, the first step to change is awareness, and the second is action.

This book aims to be more than just a discussion on corruption. It's a call to action. By understanding how it affects us, by seeing it in our daily lives, we can start to unravel its grip on our country. Each one of us can play a part in building a fairer, more transparent India.

This outline and content are designed to be relatable, simple, and actionable for every Indian who deals with corruption in daily life. By focusing on common experiences, real-life examples, and offering hope for change, it's structured to keep the reader engaged and empowered.

Chapter 11

Solutions for a Corruption-Free India

Empowering Citizens with Transparency

Transparency is a powerful tool in the fight against corruption. When citizens have access to information about how funds are used, where taxes go, and how decisions are made, they become empowered to demand accountability. Imagine a system where government projects, budgets, and spending are all available for public scrutiny. This kind of openness can act as a deterrent for those who might consider abusing their power.

One way to enhance transparency is through digital platforms that allow people to track government spending, report cases of corruption, and access information about public officials. As citizens become more informed, they also become more powerful, creating a society where corruption has fewer places to hide.

The Power of Community Action

Change doesn't only come from the top down—it also rises from communities. Local movements, neighborhood groups, and citizen-led initiatives can create environments that reject corruption. When people stand together against bribery and unfair practices, they make it clear that corruption is unacceptable.

Community action could mean reporting bribery in local offices, exposing corrupt officials, or organizing to demand better services. Small acts of resistance and accountability, multiplied across communities, have the potential to shift the cultural mindset. People start to see themselves not as powerless individuals but as part of a larger movement for integrity.

Technology as a Weapon Against Corruption

Technology has transformed nearly every aspect of modern life, and its potential to fight corruption is immense. Digital tools like mobile applications, online reporting platforms, and blockchain for transparent transactions can make corrupt practices much harder to conceal. India's growing tech landscape offers opportunities to build platforms that facilitate reporting, auditing, and tracking government actions.

For instance, in some regions, apps allow citizens to anonymously report bribes, while other technologies are being developed to track public spending in real time. The anonymity and accessibility of digital platforms mean that anyone, regardless of status, can participate in the fight against corruption. By using technology as a tool for transparency, India can take meaningful steps toward building a corruption-free society.

Conclusion: A Vision for a New India

The dream of a corruption-free India isn't just wishful thinking; it's a vision worth fighting for. With each passing day, more Indians are joining the fight, raising their voices, and refusing to accept bribes or pay them. This isn't just about laws or policies; it's about rewriting the story of a nation that values justice and integrity above all.

Imagine an India where children grow up without having to pay for basic services, where businesses compete fairly, and where leaders are chosen for their values rather than their wallets. It's a future where every citizen plays a role in shaping the nation's destiny. Yes, the path is long, and the journey is difficult, but India is moving forward, driven by the spirit of its people, and the hope that someday, corruption will be a chapter in history rather than the present reality.

This journey toward a corruption-free India is about more than policy change—it's about a cultural awakening, a shift in values, and a collective decision to choose honesty over convenience, justice over wealth, and unity over division. Together, India can stand tall, reclaiming its promise of fairness, opportunity, and dignity for all.

Chapter 12

Taking Action – The Role of Every Citizen

The Power of Individual Choices

Every single choice a person makes can impact the larger fight against corruption. From refusing to pay small bribes to speaking out against unethical practices in the workplace, each action matters. Imagine a marketplace where buyers and sellers engage in fair practices, or a public office where everyone stands in line, refusing to pay under-the-table fees. These small acts of integrity, multiplied by millions of Indians, can set the groundwork for a lasting transformation.

It's easy to feel that individual actions won't make a difference, but change always starts with one person standing up and choosing a different path. When enough individuals decide to say "no" to corruption, they create a ripple effect that spreads through families, workplaces, and communities, reaching the highest levels of government.

A Collective Responsibility

Ending corruption in India isn't a task for the government alone; it's a responsibility shared by every citizen. Families, schools, religious institutions, and media all play a role in fostering a culture that values honesty and integrity. Imagine communities where children are raised with stories of courage and justice, where students learn about the importance of ethical choices, and where leaders are celebrated not for their wealth but for their integrity.

Creating such a culture is not easy, but it's essential for a healthy society. When people hold one another accountable, they build a network of support that can withstand the temptations of corruption. By taking collective responsibility, Indians can work together to build a stronger, more unified country.

The Road Ahead: Sustained Effort for Lasting Change

The journey toward a corruption-free India is not one that will be completed overnight. It requires sustained effort, patience, and a commitment that spans generations. Just as corruption didn't appear overnight, it won't disappear in a day. But with persistence, India can create a future where integrity becomes the norm, not the exception.

Every time an Indian chooses integrity, every time someone decides to report a corrupt act, they're contributing to a better future. These actions may seem small individually, but together, they form the foundation of a transformed India. This journey, fueled by the hopes, dreams, and actions of millions, will lead to a nation where corruption no longer holds power, and where every citizen can live with dignity and pride.

Conclusion: Building a New India, Together

As we close this exploration of corruption and its impact, remember that every story of struggle has the potential to become a story of victory. The path toward a corruption-free India is challenging, but with each step, the country moves closer to a brighter future. It's a journey that calls for courage, resilience, and a vision that reaches beyond individual gain to the well-being of every citizen.

Imagine an India where trust in government is restored, where businesses thrive on fair practices, and where citizens feel safe, valued, and proud. This vision is possible if every Indian commits to integrity and honesty in their daily lives. Together, India can reclaim its promise as a nation built on principles, where fairness and justice are not just ideals but realities. This is the India we must strive to build—one where future generations can look back and see a legacy of courage, unity, and unwavering commitment to what is right.

FAQs

1. Why is corruption so deeply rooted in India?

Corruption in India has historical roots, driven by economic inequalities, complex bureaucratic processes, and, at times, a lack of accountability. Over time, it has become ingrained in many aspects of society, often seen as a "necessary evil" to navigate certain systems. Tackling corruption requires addressing these root causes, along with cultural changes and stronger enforcement of laws.

2. How can ordinary citizens contribute to fighting corruption?

Ordinary citizens have a powerful role in the fight against corruption. By refusing to pay bribes, reporting unethical practices, and supporting transparent policies, they can help create a culture of accountability. Simple acts of integrity, when multiplied by millions, can lead to meaningful change.

3. Are there any examples of successful anti-corruption efforts in India?

Yes, there have been various successful initiatives in India. For example, digitalization of government services has reduced opportunities for bribes, and organizations like the Central Vigilance Commission work to promote accountability. In some states, citizen-led initiatives and mobile apps allow individuals to report corruption anonymously, fostering greater transparency.

4. How does corruption affect India's economy?

Corruption has a significant impact on the economy by stifling innovation, discouraging foreign investment, and diverting resources away from public services. Funds meant for infrastructure, healthcare, and education often end up in the hands of corrupt officials, affecting the quality of life for millions of Indians and slowing down economic growth.

5. What role does education play in fighting corruption?

Education is critical in the fight against corruption. By teaching values like honesty, accountability, and empathy from a young age, schools can help foster a generation that values integrity over personal gain. Informed and aware youth are more likely to question unethical practices and advocate for a fair and just society.

By understanding the pervasive nature of corruption and committing to collective action, every Indian can be part of a movement to create a just, equitable, and transparent nation. The journey is long, but the destination—a corruption-free India—is well worth the effort. Together, step by step, India can and will overcome the darkness of corruption, lighting the way for future generations to live in a country they can proudly call their own.

A Final Call to Action: Lighting the Flame of Change

Imagine an India where people no longer fear being cheated, where dreams aren't thwarted by a corrupt system, and where fairness flows as naturally as the rivers that sustain our land. This is not just a distant dream—it is the India that every one of us can help create.

When we think of India's greatness, we remember the strength of our diversity, our spirit of resilience, and the profound wisdom passed down through generations. These values have been the backbone of our society, guiding us through centuries of challenges and triumphs. Yet corruption has cast a shadow over our nation, dulling the brilliance that India is meant to shine with. The good news? We have the power to reclaim this light.

A Shared Vision of Hope

This journey towards an India free from corruption doesn't have to be a lonely one. It's a collective path, where every step forward represents not just one person's actions but the spirit of a united nation. When a teacher chooses to model integrity, when a government official decides to serve honestly, or when a young entrepreneur builds a business with transparent practices, each of these actions becomes a beacon of hope. These choices echo through society, showing others that it is possible to live by values even in a world where many choose shortcuts.

Let's embrace the vision of a fair India as a common purpose—a purpose that drives us to raise our children with the understanding that honesty is not just the best policy but the only policy. This vision can live in every family conversation, in every classroom discussion, and in every community gathering, reminding us of our shared responsibility to create a nation built on integrity.

Empowering Each Generation

Each generation has the opportunity to correct the mistakes of the past. To today's youth—the generation blessed with information and connectivity like never before—the torch of this movement belongs to you. You have the power to demand transparency, to hold leaders accountable, and to use technology as a tool for truth. In your hands lies the strength to shape an India that rewards hard work over influence and integrity over wealth.

To the parents, teachers, and mentors: it is within your reach to guide this next generation toward an India that refuses to compromise on principles. By sharing stories of honesty and kindness, by celebrating those who stand against corruption, and by setting examples in your own lives, you help sow the seeds of a brighter future.

A Legacy of Integrity

Imagine an India where future generations look back at this time as the turning point—a moment in history when the people chose honesty over corruption, unity over division, and hope over despair. Together, we can create this legacy. Let's write this story of India with our choices, our courage, and our collective will.

The power to eradicate corruption doesn't lie in the hands of a few but in the collective will of a billion hearts. This isn't just about laws and policies; it's about nurturing a culture where every Indian, regardless of their background, can hold their head high, proud to be part of a nation that values truth and justice.

This is our India. This is our moment. Let us walk together toward a future where the light of integrity shines bright and unwavering, inspiring generations to come.

Thank you for taking this journey through the complexities of corruption and the strength of a nation determined to rise above it. India's future is in our hands—one choice, one action, one day at a time.

"The India of our dreams is within reach. Stand with integrity, act with courage, and together, we will create a legacy of justice and unity."

A New Dawn for India: Embracing a Future of Integrity

As we reach the end of this journey, it's important to reflect on the true spirit of India—the spirit that has withstood centuries of challenges, yet continues to shine. This spirit, deeply rooted in values of honesty, compassion, and resilience, has always been India's guiding light. Corruption may have dimmed this light in recent years, but it can never extinguish it. Now, more than ever, we stand on the brink of a new dawn—a dawn we can welcome with our collective choice to change.

The Time to Act is Now

The fight against corruption is no longer something we can postpone or leave to others. The time to act is now, with each of us playing our part, however big or small. Every time we refuse to give in to corruption, every time we support fair practices, and every time we stand up for what's right, we contribute to a culture of integrity that no force can undermine.

It's not easy to break free from the chains of corruption, especially when it's ingrained in so many aspects of daily life. But real change never comes easy. Like the freedom fighters who faced unimaginable hardships for India's independence, we, too, must summon the courage to face today's challenge. Only by pushing through discomfort and confronting the deep-seated habits of corruption can we truly break free and create an India that lives up to its potential.

Honouring Our Heroes Through Our Actions

As Indians, we proudly remember the sacrifices of our heroes, from Gandhi to Bhagat Singh, who fought not just for freedom but for a country founded on justice and equality. Honoring their legacy means building a society that reflects those same values. Imagine an India where everyone can achieve success through hard work, where government officials serve the people with dedication, and where communities uplift each other without prejudice or greed.

Each of us has a hero within—a voice that urges us to do what's right, to stand firm, and to act with integrity. When we listen to this voice, we honor not only our ancestors but also the generations that will follow. Let our actions today be a source of pride for tomorrow's India.

The Power of Unity: Together, We Can Make History

There is strength in unity, and when we come together as a people, our power is boundless. Imagine a society where every citizen, regardless of age, background, or wealth, feels responsible for the nation's well-being. Imagine students organizing anti-corruption rallies, businesses pledging to practice fair trade, families instilling values of honesty, and communities standing against injustice together. This is the vision of India that can become a reality when we unite in our fight against corruption.

When one person stands alone against corruption, it's difficult. But when millions stand together, demanding fairness, transparency, and accountability, they form an unstoppable force. Together, we can make history—an era when corruption was defeated, and India emerged stronger, more vibrant, and more just than ever before.

Leaving a Legacy of Hope and Honor

One day, generations will look back on this time, perhaps reading these very words, and they will remember this as the moment when India chose to rise. Let's leave a legacy that fills them with pride, a legacy where honor triumphed over greed, where truth prevailed over deceit, and where justice was not just a word but a way of life.

Let's not underestimate the power of hope, the strength of unity, and the impact of integrity. This is our moment to shape India's future. Each choice we make, every honest act, and every refusal to participate in corruption adds to a larger movement that will echo across the ages. Together, we are writing the story of a new India—an India that stands as a beacon of integrity for the world to see.

Thank you for being part of this journey. Remember, the battle against corruption may be challenging, but it is a battle worth fighting. With courage, unity, and an unbreakable spirit, we will see the India of our dreams come to life—a nation that stands tall, free from corruption, and strong in its unwavering values.

Together, let's create an India that shines brighter with each passing day, lighting the path for future generations to walk with pride, purpose, and hope.

One Final Word:
Believe in the Power of Change

In this journey against corruption, there's one truth we must carry forward: change is possible. History is full of stories where seemingly insurmountable challenges were overcome by people who refused to accept the world as it was. India's own story is a testament to this—the courage, sacrifice, and relentless hope that gave birth to our freedom are woven into the fabric of our identity.

Today, we face a different battle. It's not one fought with weapons or against a visible oppressor, but it's a struggle for integrity, for fairness, and for the soul of our nation. And just like in the past, this fight calls for people with unwavering determination, people who are willing to stand up for a cause that transcends their own lives.

The Ripple Effect: How One Act Inspires Another

Never underestimate the impact of a single action. Imagine that every time one person chooses integrity over dishonesty, it creates a ripple—a ripple that grows and spreads, touching lives and inspiring others. Picture a shop owner who decides to run his business with honesty. His customers notice, respect him, and maybe even follow his example. Picture a young student who, after reading about the heroes of the anti-corruption movement, decides she will never accept a bribe, no matter the circumstances. Her friends hear her resolve and are inspired to take the same stance. And so, the ripple continues, extending from individuals to families, communities, and, eventually, the nation as a whole.

This ripple effect is how revolutions start. It's how the spirit of change sweeps across nations and transforms societies. Believe that your actions matter because they do. Believe that your choices will inspire others because they will. Each time you stand for what's right, you're lighting a flame that grows stronger, that will one day illuminate the entire nation.

A Promise to Future Generations

Think about the kind of India we want to leave for our children and grandchildren. Do we want them to live in a country where they're constantly forced to navigate corruption, where dreams are sacrificed because of unethical practices? Or do we want to build an India where they can pursue their aspirations without fear, where fairness prevails, and where every citizen has an equal chance to succeed?

This is our promise to future generations: a country where they can grow up proud, free from the chains of dishonesty and exploitation. Our actions today will determine the kind of world they inherit tomorrow. Let's make sure it's a world they're proud to call home.

The Strength of Hope: Together, We Will Prevail

Hope is a powerful force, one that can lift entire nations out of darkness. The journey toward a corruption-free India may be long and difficult, but hope is what keeps us going. It's the belief that better days lie ahead, that with each step forward, we're closer to a future where corruption is a relic of the past.

So let us keep hope alive. Let it be the foundation of this movement and the fuel for our actions. When things get tough, when we feel like giving up, let hope remind us of why we started this journey in the first place.

The Time Has Come: Let's Rewrite India's Story

This is the moment. The pages of India's story are open before us, waiting for the next chapter to be written. Let's fill those pages with stories of courage, resilience, and unity. Let's tell a story of a people who refused to be broken by corruption, who stood together and created an India that reflects the best of humanity.

This is the legacy we have the power to create. Let's be the generation that turned the tide, that chose integrity over convenience, that believed in a vision of India that's free, fair, and just. It won't be easy, but if we hold on to hope, if we keep our hearts united, there is nothing we cannot achieve.

So, let us walk forward, hand in hand, with the light of integrity as our guide. Let's build an India that shines not only for us but for generations to come. An India where honesty is celebrated, where every citizen feels valued, and where the dream of a just nation is finally realized.

Together, let's make history. Let's create the India of our dreams.

Thank you for believing, for caring, and for taking each step forward in this journey toward a brighter, corruption-free India. Let's carry this vision in our hearts, for the India we create today will be the foundation of tomorrow's legacy.

A Courageous Journey Forward: Your Role in India's Future

As we stand at the threshold of change, one thing is clear: this journey is one that demands courage. The courage to speak up when silence would be easier. The courage to choose honesty when the world around us may seem indifferent. The courage to be a part of something bigger than ourselves.

Imagine what India could be—a place where our neighbours, colleagues, friends, and family live free of the fear and frustration that corruption breeds. A place where we walk into government offices knowing we will be treated fairly, where businesses compete honourably, and where children grow up with dreams that are no longer hindered by unfair barriers. This is an India worth fighting for, and it starts with each of us taking responsibility.

The Power of a Collective Stand

Each of us has the power to make a difference, and when we stand together, our strength multiplies. Perhaps you wonder what one person can achieve, but remember, every movement in history began with a single spark—a spark that caught the wind and became an unstoppable force. That spark lives within each of us today. Our collective voices, our united actions, and our shared commitment to a just India will send a resounding message that we, the people, will no longer tolerate corruption.

The journey may be challenging, and there may be moments of doubt. But let us remind ourselves that courage isn't the absence of fear—it's the resolve to keep going despite it. And when we join hands, lifting each other in times of need, we'll find the strength to overcome any obstacle.

The Legacy We Leave Behind

What legacy do we want to leave behind? The answer to that question lies within our hearts. A legacy is more than just a memory; it's a living example for those who follow. When future generations look back at this era, let them see us as the generation that chose integrity over convenience, unity over division, and truth over corruption.

Let them see us as the generation that dared to believe in a brighter India and took courageous steps to bring that vision to life. Let's build a foundation on which our children can stand proudly, knowing that they belong to a nation that values honor, fairness, and justice.

An Unbreakable Spirit: The India We Dream Of

This dream of a better India is no longer just an idea. It is a promise, a commitment, a movement. And it's growing stronger each day. As we face each new day, let's carry this vision in our hearts and minds. Let's remind ourselves that the India we dream of is worth every sacrifice, every challenge, and every effort we make.

Our spirit is unbreakable, our hope unwavering, and our vision of a corruption-free India is clear. Together, let's keep moving forward with determination, carrying the torch of honesty and justice. We are not alone in this journey; we walk with millions of others who share the same dream. Let's continue to inspire, support, and encourage one another, knowing that with each step, we are closer to realizing the India of our dreams.

Let's Make History Together

In the end, this journey isn't just about fighting corruption—it's about creating a new chapter in India's story. It's about building a nation that reflects our highest values, our deepest beliefs, and our collective strength. This is the history we have the power to create, and it starts with you, with me, with all of us.

So let's write this chapter together, with courage in our hearts and hope lighting our way. Let's make history, not just for ourselves but for every generation that will call this country home. The India we dream of is within our reach, and it's up to us to bring it to life.

Thank you for being part of this vision. Let's walk together toward an India that stands as a beacon of integrity, justice, and unity. Our journey has just begun, and our spirit will carry us forward until we see the dawn of a truly corruption-free India.

Together, let's make history. Let's create a legacy. Let's bring the India of our dreams to life.

A Final Promise: Carry the Flame of Change

As we reach the end of this message, let us hold on to the vision of a fair and just India—a vision so vibrant that it moves us beyond words into meaningful action. The path we are on isn't easy, but it's one worth traveling. With each honest choice we make, each act of integrity, and every time we say "no" to corruption, we are fueling a movement far greater than ourselves.

This movement isn't just a fight against corruption; it's a rallying call to reclaim the India we know in our hearts to be possible. When you wake each day, carry this flame of change with you. Let it be a reminder of the legacy we are building, of the promises we are keeping—not just to ourselves but to every Indian who believes in a nation of integrity.

Believing in a Brighter Tomorrow

Sometimes, in the face of corruption, it can feel like change is a distant dream. Yet history tells us that great revolutions were often born in moments of doubt, when a handful of people dared to believe in something bigger. Let's hold on to that belief. When we envision a corruption-free India, we aren't just wishing for a better nation; we are setting our course towards a brighter tomorrow.

This is a tomorrow where our children won't have to fear unfair obstacles, where opportunity isn't defined by who you know, but by your ability and determination. It's a tomorrow where India's strength is built on the honesty of its citizens, the fairness of its systems, and the unity of its people. Every time we choose integrity, we draw this vision of tomorrow closer to becoming today's reality.

Lighting the Path for Generations to Come

Let this movement be a gift to the generations who will follow. The fight against corruption isn't just for us; it's for every child who will grow up in this land, every dreamer who will strive for greatness, and every citizen who deserves the dignity of a fair and just society.

Imagine the world we are building for them—a world where their worth isn't determined by wealth or influence, but by their character, dreams, and contributions to society. Imagine the pride they'll feel, knowing they belong to a country that stood up for what's right. The India we are shaping today will be a beacon for tomorrow's children, guiding them to a future rich in promise, fairness, and hope.

A Journey We Will Walk Together

This journey may test us, but we are not alone. Together, with shared purpose and unwavering conviction, we are creating a legacy of honor that will inspire and uplift us all. Each step, each small act of courage, adds to the momentum of this movement. It tells the world that India is a nation of people who will not give up, who will not turn away, and who will always choose integrity, even in the face of challenges.

Let's walk this path hand in hand, knowing that with every act of integrity, we are bringing the India we dream of into reality. As we move forward, let us remember that we have the power to change the course of history. Together, let's transform India into a country where honesty is the norm, fairness is a right, and justice is for all.

The India of Our Dreams is Within Reach

This is our India, our moment, and our movement. Let us carry this vision forward with love, hope, and an unwavering commitment to do what's right. The India of our dreams—a land where integrity reigns and every citizen walks with pride—isn't a distant hope; it's a promise we're making to ourselves and to each other.

Thank you for holding this vision close, for believing in change, and for committing to this journey. The India of our dreams is within reach. Together, we will make it real, and together, we will make history.

"India is waiting, and the power to change it lies in our hands. Let's carry this flame, and let it shine bright. For today, for tomorrow, for every generation to come."

The Call to Every Indian Heart: Be the Change, Ignite the Future

To each of you reading this, know that you are not just a part of this journey—you are its heartbeat. The future of India isn't solely in the hands of leaders or institutions; it's in the hands of every one of us who dares to believe, who dreams of an India that is honest, fair, and filled with integrity. This is a vision that transcends generations, one that has the power to inspire millions, if only we each take up the call.

Stand Tall, Stand Together

In every corner of this nation, there are people just like you who believe in change, who want a brighter future. This belief is the foundation upon which our new India will be built. Stand tall, knowing that you are part of a movement greater than any single individual—a movement built on unity, resilience, and the desire for a better tomorrow.

Every act of honesty, every decision to reject corruption, every stand you take for fairness contributes to a ripple effect that extends far beyond what any of us can see. As individuals, we may only see a small part of the change, but together, we are creating an unstoppable wave that will transform our nation from the ground up.

Believe in Your Power to Inspire

Never underestimate the power of your own influence. When you choose to live with integrity, you're not only changing your own life; you're inspiring those around you to do the same. Whether it's your family, friends, colleagues, or even strangers who witness your example, your courage to act with honor has the power to ignite change in others.

We may never know the full extent of the impact we make, but the smallest actions can light a spark in someone else's heart. Imagine an India where millions of hearts are ablaze with the same passion for honesty, fairness, and justice. That's the India we are building, one choice at a time.

Carrying the Flame Forward

As we look ahead, let's keep this flame alive. The journey may be long, but our commitment to a corruption-free India will not waver. We are the custodians of this vision, the torchbearers for a future that reflects our highest ideals. Our children, our communities, our entire nation depends on this resolve to hold the flame high, even in the face of challenges.

This flame represents not only hope but an unbreakable promise—a promise to ourselves, to our children, and to all who share in this vision. When we pass this flame forward, we pass forward our belief in a nation that embodies integrity and justice.

A Movement That Starts with You

Real change doesn't begin with laws or policies; it begins with people. It begins with you. Each time you choose to do what's right, even when no one is watching, you are reshaping India's future. You are making a difference, creating a world where integrity is the standard, not the exception.

Let this journey start within each of us. Let us be the kind of citizens that India needs, the kind of people who lift each other up, who protect each other, and who are willing to make sacrifices for the greater good. The India of our dreams depends on us. Let's rise to the occasion and be the change we seek.

Together, We Will Build a New India

This isn't just a dream; it's a reality waiting to unfold. Together, we are building an India that is strong, just, and filled with promise. We are creating a legacy that will inspire generations, a nation that will stand as a beacon of hope and integrity for the world.

The India we see today is only the beginning. With our collective efforts, our unwavering determination, and our shared vision, we are shaping a future that honors every citizen, respects every voice, and cherishes every dream. This is the India we're striving for—an India where honesty and courage are celebrated, where every child can grow up proud of the land they call home.

Take the First Step Today

So, let this be our call to action: Today, take the first step toward the India of our dreams. Refuse to compromise your values. Inspire others with your example. Stand together with your fellow citizens in unity and purpose. Let's make our voices heard, let's let our actions speak, and let's bring our vision of a corruption-free India to life.

The journey may be long, but our spirit is strong. The India we dream of is within our reach, and together, we will make it real.

Thank you for being a part of this vision. Thank you for believing in change. And thank you for walking this path with hope, honor, and courage.

This is our moment. Let's seize it. Let's build an India that future generations will be proud to inherit. Together, we will change history. Together, we will create a legacy that shines for all time.

This is our promise, our commitment, and our legacy. For the India we cherish, for the future we envision, and for every Indian who believes in the power of change—let's move forward with hope and purpose. The journey has just begun, and together, we will make it a journey of triumph, integrity, and unity.

A Final Call to Action: Let's Build India Together

As you read these words, feel the weight of this truth—**India's future rests in our hands.** We are the architects of the change we so desperately need. We are the ones who can turn this dream of a fair, just, and corruption-free nation into reality. But for that, we must stand up and act. The journey ahead is challenging, but every step we take together will bring us closer to the India we all desire.

Our Power Lies in Our Unity

This is not a battle that can be fought alone. It is a collective effort—a unified push toward what's right. But in that unity lies our greatest strength. When we join hands, we become unstoppable. When we speak with one voice, our message echoes far and wide. And when we each take individual responsibility to do what's right, we ignite a change that ripples across the nation.

Let us be the voices that inspire others. Let us be the hands that reach out to those who are struggling. Let us be the hearts that never give up on our vision for a corruption-free India. The fight for integrity is not just a fight for our generation, but for the generations that will follow. Our children, our grandchildren—**they will thank us for standing up today.**

Empowerment Starts with Action

It's easy to feel powerless in the face of corruption, to think that our individual efforts don't matter. But I promise you, every small act of courage counts. Every time you reject the temptation to give or receive a bribe, every time you speak up against injustice, you are contributing to a powerful change. It may not seem like much in the moment, but over time, these acts create a tidal wave of transformation.

Imagine the power we hold in our hands: the power to shape our nation with our actions, our choices, our voices. Imagine the power we have to inspire one another, to lift each other up, to build an India where truth and justice reign. This is our moment to stand tall. This is our time to choose what kind of country we want to live in.

We Are Stronger Than Corruption

Corruption may seem all-encompassing, but it is no match for the strength and resilience of the people. **We are stronger than corruption.** We are more united than the forces that seek to divide us. And we are more determined than those who think they can keep us down.

Every act of resistance against corruption is a victory. Every moment we choose integrity over convenience is a triumph. **When we unite, we become a force that no amount of corruption can withstand.**

A Better Future Awaits Us

The India we dream of is not some far-off fantasy—it is a future that is just waiting for us to claim it. A future where our streets are safe, our children are educated, and every citizen has access to the resources they need to thrive. A future where the only thing that matters is the merit of our actions and the strength of our character.

But we cannot wait for change to come from the top. **We are the change.** The power is in our hands, and it is time to embrace that power. It's time to lead by example, to be the ones who set the standard for what's right and good. This is the India we can create—a place of opportunity, fairness, and integrity.

The Road to a Corruption-Free India

This journey we are on may be long and difficult, but it is one that is worth every step. We may stumble, we may face setbacks, but we cannot afford to give up. **We are in this together.** And as long as we continue to take those steps—no matter how small—they will add up to a powerful transformation.

Let's not wait for others to make the first move. Let's be the change-makers. Let's show our children what it means to live with honor, to stand up for what's right, and to never back down in the face of adversity. Let's create an India that we can all be proud of.

Your Moment is Now

As you finish reading this, know that this is your moment. **This is your call to action.** The journey to a corruption-free India begins with you.

Ask yourself: What can I do today? What small act of courage can I take that will lead to a better India? Perhaps it's choosing honesty in the face of temptation. Maybe it's raising your voice against injustice. Or perhaps it's simply setting an example for those around you.

The change starts with us, right here, right now. Together, we will turn this dream into reality.

We are the India of Tomorrow.

Let's rise together. Let's stand firm. Let's build an India that is strong, fair, and free from the chains of corruption. **This is our time. This is our India.**

Together, let's change the world.

Thank you for believing in this vision. Thank you for standing up for a better future. Let's carry this vision forward, and let it be the legacy we leave behind for generations to come. **India is waiting. Let's answer that call with all the courage and conviction we have.**

The Time for Change is Now

We can no longer afford to sit back and wait for someone else to make the first move. **The time for change is now.** Every day that we allow corruption to thrive is a day we allow injustice to spread, a day we deny the very essence of what this great country stands for: equality, justice, and opportunity for all.

What Will You Do?

This is a moment to reflect. **What will you do today to fight corruption?** Will you take the easy road, or will you choose the path of courage, the path of integrity? I know that it's hard. I know that the systems in place can feel overwhelming, and that the voices of those seeking power and privilege often drown out the cries for justice. But we, the people of India, have always been stronger than any system—**because the power of the people is far greater than any individual or institution.**

This moment, this very second, is a chance for us to decide what kind of India we want to build. Do we want an India where power is given to the few at the cost of the many, or do we want an India where every citizen, regardless of their wealth or background, has an equal chance to succeed?

The Heartbeat of Change

The heartbeat of change begins with us. The change we seek isn't something that will be handed to us—it's something we have to take. It's not a distant dream; it's a tangible reality waiting to be claimed. We must reach for it, together, with every ounce of strength and conviction we have.

As you read these words, feel the weight of this responsibility. It is a burden, yes, but it is a burden we bear with pride. Because **this is our chance to create the India we know we deserve.**

Every small action counts. Every refusal to participate in bribery, every voice raised in protest against corruption, every act of kindness and fairness—it all matters. And when we stand united, when we walk side by side, there is no force on earth that can stop us from achieving this vision.

A Future for Our Children

Think about the future for a moment. What do we want our children to inherit? Do we want them to grow up in a world where the rich and powerful continue to exploit the weak and vulnerable? Or do we want them to live in a world where hard work, integrity, and fairness are the cornerstones of society?

The answer is clear. We want an India where our children can thrive, free from the shadows of corruption. A country where they can dream without fear, where they know that their future is not determined by their connections, but by their abilities. **We owe this to them.**

You Have the Power

I want you to hear this, deeply and personally: **You have the power to make a difference.** You may feel small in the face of corruption, but your actions have the power to ripple out and inspire others. Together, we can build a future where integrity is celebrated, where every citizen has an equal chance, and where justice is not a privilege for the few, but a right for all.

There is no action too small. There is no voice too quiet. We are all part of this change, and the smallest step you take can lead to a revolution. **The power to change India is within you.**

The India We Deserve

The India we deserve is not one of despair, but one of hope. It's a place where the corrupt are held accountable, where every citizen has the freedom to live with dignity, where justice isn't just a word, but a practice. **This is the India we deserve.**

We can't afford to wait for others to do the work. We must take responsibility for our country, for our future, and for the generations that will follow us. **This is our time.**

We must choose to rise. We must choose to fight for what is right. We must choose to act with courage, even when it's hard, even when it's unpopular. The India of our dreams is waiting for us—**but it will only become a reality if we choose to make it happen.**

A Lasting Legacy

Imagine the legacy we can leave behind—a nation where integrity is the bedrock of society, where corruption is nothing but a distant memory. Imagine the pride we will feel, knowing that we were the ones who stood up, who chose to fight, who decided that enough was enough.

This legacy isn't just about policies or institutions—it's about people. It's about each of us choosing to act with honor, to live with dignity, and to protect the values we hold dear. **This is the India we will leave behind.**

We Are the Change

So let us stand, shoulder to shoulder, with unwavering commitment. Let us stand together, because we know that we are stronger than any obstacle. The fight for a corruption-free India isn't easy, but it is worth every ounce of effort. **We are the change we seek.**

This is a moment that will define us. And when history looks back on this time, it will say: **India chose to rise. India chose integrity. India chose unity.**

And we will know that we were a part of that change. We will know that we stood together, that we fought for what was right, and that we never gave up on our vision for a better India.

The time is now. The power is ours. Let's build the India of our dreams. Together.

A Vision for India's Future

Imagine, for a moment, what India could look like without corruption. **An India where our children can grow up in a world that honors merit and hard work, where integrity is the currency of our society, and where fairness is not a distant dream, but a daily reality.**

It's not a far-off fantasy; it's a vision we can turn into reality. But it starts with us. It starts with you and me, deciding today that we will no longer be complicit in the systems that tear our nation apart.

We can look around and see the struggles, the unfairness, the system that has, for too long, allowed the corrupt to thrive while the honest suffer. But we must refuse to accept that as our reality. **This is not the India we were meant to inherit.**

We were meant to inherit an India where justice prevails, where the rule of law stands strong, where every person, no matter their background, has the opportunity to succeed. **This is the India we deserve.** And the good news is that it is within our reach. Together, we can build it.

It's Not Too Late

It's easy to feel discouraged, to think that the system is too broken, the corruption too deeply entrenched. But here's the truth: **it's not too late.** The very fact that we're having this conversation, that we're asking questions, and that we're seeking a better way forward means there is hope.

This isn't a lost cause. Change is difficult, but it is possible. Every revolution, every significant change in history, began with people just like you, who chose to stand up and speak out. The road to justice may be long, but **every step forward is a victory.**

If we stand together—if we, as citizens of this incredible country, decide to come together with unwavering resolve—**nothing can stop us.**

The Strength of Our Resolve

What makes us so powerful as a people is not just the strength of our will but the strength of our unity. When we come together with a shared vision, with a collective purpose, we become unstoppable. **We are stronger than corruption.** We are stronger than the challenges we face. We are stronger than the voices that tell us to give up.

It's easy to feel isolated when we're standing against corruption, but we must remember: **We are not alone.** Every time we choose integrity over compromise, we are connecting with countless others across India who are doing the same. We are creating a network of change, one decision at a time.

Together, we will rise.

Honesty is Our Strength

At the heart of this battle is one simple truth: **honesty is our greatest strength.** It may seem like a small thing, an insignificant gesture to choose honesty in a world that often rewards dishonesty, but it is anything but small. Each time we choose to be honest, each time we refuse to participate in a corrupt system, we are taking one more step toward transforming our country.

It's easy to get disillusioned, to think that the battle is already lost. But we must believe in the power of small actions. **Small actions lead to big change.**

The truth is, change begins within. When we choose to live with integrity, when we make those difficult decisions to do what's right even when no one is watching, we become the leaders we need. **We lead by example.**

A Call to Every Citizen

This is a call to every single citizen of India: **We need you.** Whether you're a teacher, a farmer, a student, a worker, or a business leader—you have a role to play in this transformation. Your actions matter. The choices you make, the values you uphold, the example you set—these all play a part in shaping the India we are working toward.

We are not waiting for others to change. We are **the change we seek.** Each of us has the power to make a difference. It starts with you. It starts with me. It starts with all of us.

Let's Stand United for a Better India

India has always been a land of resilience, of strength, and of hope. When we unite, when we stand together, there is no force that can stop us. Let us draw from the strength of our ancestors, from the lessons of our past, and from the burning desire we have for a brighter, better future.

We are stronger than we know. We are united in our resolve. Together, we will create a nation that we can all be proud of. A nation where corruption no longer holds power over us. A nation where justice is not a privilege but a right.

This is our moment. This is our fight. And together, we will win.

A Legacy of Integrity

What will your legacy be? Will you be a part of the generation that stood by and watched as corruption stole the heart of India, or will you be the one who said enough is enough? Will you stand in the shadows, or will you stand in the light, fighting for what's right?

This is your moment. The India we leave behind will be defined by the actions we take today. Will we leave behind a nation shackled by corruption, or will we leave a legacy of integrity, honor, and justice?

The choice is ours.

The Road Ahead

The road ahead will not be easy. It will be full of challenges, setbacks, and obstacles. But we are not afraid of the struggle. **We are the people of India, and we are strong.**

Every fight for justice is a fight worth having. Every step toward a corruption-free India is a step worth taking. Every sacrifice we make for the greater good will echo through generations. And when we look back on this journey, we will know that we were part of something bigger than ourselves.

We will know that we did not give up. We will know that we gave everything to make India the nation we always knew it could be.

Together, we will succeed. Together, we will build a better India. **And together, we will change the world.**

This is our mission. This is our future. Let's rise, together, and make India the shining example of what a nation can be when its people stand united against corruption. **The time for change is now.** Let's make it happen.

A Future We Can Build Together

The India we dream of isn't a distant fantasy—**it is a vision within our reach**. With every step we take, with every decision to act with integrity, we are building that future. But we can't do it alone. **We need each other**. The strength of our nation lies not in the wealth or power of a few individuals, but in the hearts and minds of every citizen, working together toward a common goal.

We've seen how powerful corruption can be, how it seeps into every facet of our society. But what we've also seen is the extraordinary resilience of the people of India—the courage to rise up, to demand change, and to fight for a better future.

We are more powerful than corruption. Together, we can take back the future we deserve. **Together, we can break free from the chains that have held us back for so long.**

From Every Corner of India, A Unified Voice

It doesn't matter where you come from—whether you live in a bustling city or a small village, whether you have wealth or struggle to make ends meet. **This fight belongs to all of us**. The voices of millions of Indians, united by the desire for justice and fairness, will create a roar so loud that it cannot be ignored.

India is a land of diverse cultures, religions, languages, and traditions. Yet, we are united by a common thread: **our love for our country, our yearning for justice, and our hope for a future free from the poison of corruption.** The forces of greed and power have divided us for far too long, but now is the time to come together, stronger than ever before. **Our unity will be our greatest weapon.**

It Starts with Us—One Act of Courage at a Time

Change is never easy. It's never without sacrifice. But every time we choose to do what's right, no matter the consequences, we are taking a step closer to the India we deserve.

It all starts with us. It starts with the courage to stand up in the face of injustice, to turn down a bribe, to report corruption when we see it, and to speak out when others are too afraid to do so. Each of these actions may seem small on its own, but when they are multiplied by the millions of Indians who are willing to take them, they become a movement—a tidal wave of change that will wash away the corruption that has plagued our nation for far too long.

You might think, "What difference can one person make?" But history has shown us time and time again that **one person can change the world**. It only takes one spark to ignite a fire. It only takes one voice to start a revolution. **You are that spark. You are that voice.**

The Strength of Our People

The Indian people have always been strong. **We've fought for independence. We've weathered countless storms.** And every time, we've come out stronger. Corruption is no match for our spirit. We are resilient, we are determined, and we will not stop until we see our country thrive.

Think about all the incredible things we've accomplished—**despite the odds stacked against us**. Think about the resilience of farmers, the sacrifices of teachers, the dreams of students, and the hopes of parents who want nothing more than a better future for their children. This is the India that exists in the hearts of every citizen: an India that works hard, that believes in justice, that refuses to be held back by the forces of corruption.

This is the India that will rise.

What Will We Leave Behind?

The legacy we leave behind matters. What will the world say about us? What will our children say about the choices we made? Will they look back and wonder why we allowed corruption to continue, or will they see a generation that chose to fight, to take a stand, and to create a future where integrity and fairness reign?

We cannot afford to leave behind a country where corruption is the norm. We cannot allow future generations to inherit a broken system. We must be the generation that stands up and says, "**Enough.**"

This is our chance to create the legacy of a lifetime—a legacy of integrity, of justice, and of hope. **We will not be remembered as a generation that stood by and did nothing. We will be remembered as the generation that fought for change.**

It's Time to Dream Again

India's potential is limitless. But we can never reach it if we allow corruption to continue unchecked. **We must dream again—dream of an India where every citizen can live in dignity, where every child has access to education, where every person has a fair chance to succeed.**

This is the dream worth fighting for.

Imagine a country where our roads are safe, our hospitals provide care without discrimination, and our institutions are built on trust. Picture a place where fairness is not just a concept but a way of life. **We can build this India, but it starts with us.**

An Invitation to Act

Today, I'm asking you to join this fight. I'm asking you to be part of something greater than yourself—**to be part of the movement that will transform India into a country free of corruption, a country where integrity is the highest form of currency.**

This is not just a book you're reading. This is a call to action. **This is the moment when you choose what kind of India you want to live in.**

The Power of One

I want to leave you with this: **The power of one is immense.** One person can start a movement. One person can change the course of history. **You have that power.**

Do not underestimate the power of your choices. **You can change the future.**

And it starts with you.

A Better India Awaits

In the end, we know that the road ahead will not be easy. There will be challenges. There will be times when the system seems impossible to change. But we have something more powerful than any obstacle: **our belief in what is right.**

And as long as we hold onto that belief, as long as we continue to fight with everything we have, there is nothing we cannot overcome. Together, we will build a better India. **An India that is free from corruption, where justice prevails, and where every citizen can thrive.**

The time is now. The change begins with us.

Let's rise together. Let's be the change. Let's build the India we know is possible.

The Light at the End of the Tunnel

When we look at the future, it might seem distant and uncertain. At times, the fight against corruption can feel like an endless battle. But I promise you, **there is light at the end of the tunnel**. We may be walking through a storm, but we are not walking alone.

This is our time to stand tall—to rise up against the darkness that corruption has cast upon us. Every single effort, every sacrifice, every act of honesty, no matter how small, **brings us closer to that light.** With every action we take, we are carving a path toward a brighter, cleaner India.

This light is not just a dream; it is the future we are building, brick by brick. We are the architects of this future, and we cannot afford to lose hope now. No matter how heavy the burden, no matter how fierce the opposition, we will keep moving forward.

Hope for Our Children

Imagine a world where our children can live without fear of bribery and corruption. A world where they don't have to compromise their morals to survive. **That is the world we must fight for.**

As parents, as citizens, as guardians of the next generation, **we owe it to them to fight for a better world**. We owe them an India where they can dream freely, where their future is not marred by the taint of corruption, but is instead a shining example of what can happen when integrity leads the way.

This fight is for them. Every child who looks up at us with hope in their eyes deserves the opportunity to grow up in a world where fairness and justice reign. **Every child who dreams of a better future deserves to have that dream realized.**

And we, the adults, the leaders, and the citizens, are the ones who must make that future possible. **It is our responsibility to leave behind a world where they can thrive without fear.**

The Power of Collective Action

Each of us has the power to make a difference. But when we come together, we become a force to be reckoned with. **There is no power stronger than a united people.**

Together, we can change the systems that have held us back. Together, we can dismantle the web of corruption that has woven itself into every corner of our society. Together, we can build something better. **We are stronger than corruption. We are stronger than fear.**

This is not just about one person doing the right thing—**this is about a collective effort.** When millions of voices rise together, they cannot be ignored. When millions of hands work together, they create a force that no one can stop. **Together, we can bring the change we seek.**

The Power of Knowledge

Change begins with awareness. The more we understand the depth of corruption, the more equipped we are to fight it. But it's not enough to just be aware—we must act on that knowledge.

Knowledge is our weapon. The more we understand how corruption works, the more we can expose it. The more we speak out, the more we educate others, the closer we get to a corruption-free India.

Together, we can shine a light on the dark corners where corruption hides. We can hold those in power accountable. We can demand transparency. We can demand justice.

A Nation Transformed by Integrity

Picture an India where honesty is celebrated. A nation where doing the right thing is not an act of bravery, but simply the way things are done. An India where the honest man and woman are not punished, but rewarded. **This is the nation we must create.**

We are a nation of dreamers. **We are a nation of doers.** But above all, we are a nation of fighters. And we will fight for the future we deserve. **We will fight for an India where integrity is the highest virtue.**

This fight will not be won in a day. But every day that we continue to fight, every day that we choose honesty, every day that we raise our voices against corruption, is a victory. **This is the fight of our lives. And we will win it, together.**

The Change Starts Now

The future we've been waiting for is not something that will come someday—it is something we can start building **right now**. Every act of courage, every decision to stand up to corruption, every time we refuse to be complicit, we are laying the foundation for the India we want to see.

The road ahead will not be easy, and we will face many challenges. But the moment we choose to stand up, **the moment we choose to be the change**—that is the moment we take back our country. And that is the moment the future of India changes forever.

We are not waiting for someone else to make the change. **We are the change.**

A Nation That Will Rise Again

We have been knocked down. We have been defeated time and time again by the forces of corruption. But we are not broken. **We are not defeated.** We are a nation that will rise again. We will rise stronger than ever before, fueled by our dreams, our values, and our determination to create a better India.

This is our time. **We will not wait for others to act. We will act.**

Let this be the generation that stood tall, the generation that refused to be silenced, the generation that fought for the truth and for justice. Let us be the generation that turned the tide.

Together, we will rise. Together, we will create the India of our dreams.

Our Moment to Shine

We are living in a time where the decisions we make today will echo through generations. **We are the change-makers, the visionaries, the warriors of justice.** It is time for us to rise and take our place in history.

Let this be the time we look back on with pride—when we can say, **we were part of the generation that made India great again.**

Together, we will build a nation that is free from the chains of corruption. Together, we will leave behind a legacy of justice, integrity, and hope. Together, we will create the India we have always dreamed of.

The time is now. Let's rise, together.

The Heartbeat of Our Nation

In the deepest corners of our hearts, we know that **India's strength has always come from its people**. It's not the politicians or the powerful businessmen that make this country great—it is the unwavering spirit of every Indian citizen. From the farmer tilling the land in the villages to the teacher shaping minds in the cities, **India's heartbeat pulses through each of us.**

The strength of our nation is not in its wealth, but in its people's **unbreakable resilience, unyielding hope, and undeniable courage.** It's in the way we rise after every fall, how we find light in the darkest of times, and how we continue to move forward despite all the challenges in our path.

When we choose to come together, **we become unstoppable**. Each and every one of us has a part to play in the story of India's transformation. **This is our time to rise, to stand together, and to be the change we want to see.**

The Battle Is Not Over Yet

Yes, we have made progress, and yes, we have seen change. But the battle against corruption is far from over. **Corruption is like a virus—it mutates and spreads** to every corner, hiding in the shadows, trying to break the spirits of those who want to do what is right.

But here's the truth: **we are stronger than corruption.** Every time we speak out, every time we refuse to give in, every time we take a stand for integrity, we are breaking the chains that have held us captive.

Change does not happen overnight. **It happens in small, consistent steps**—when we say no to bribery, when we expose injustice, when we hold those in power accountable. **It happens when we refuse to stay silent.**

It's About More Than Just Us

The fight against corruption isn't just about improving our own lives—it's about building a better India for **everyone**. It's about the millions of children who deserve a bright future, the mothers and fathers who work tirelessly to support their families, and the young students who dream of a country where opportunities are equal for all. **We owe it to them to fight.**

Think of the India we could build—where the poor don't have to bribe their way to a government scheme, where the sick don't have to pay extra just to be treated, where the educated can get jobs based on their skills and merit, not connections. **This is the India we must fight for.**

And we, the people of India, have the power to build it. **It's within our grasp.**

The Courage to Lead by Example

True leadership isn't about titles or power—it's about the courage to lead by example. The courage to stand up for what's right, even when the world around us says it's easier to stay quiet. **True leaders are those who act with integrity** and inspire others to do the same.

Each of us has the potential to be that leader. **You don't need to hold a position of power to lead; you just need the courage to do what is right**. We can all make a difference in our own small way. When you choose honesty, when you choose fairness, you lead by example.

If we all lead by example, we will create a nation that cannot be stopped.

A New India Built on Trust

The most valuable asset we can build in this country is trust. **Trust between the people and their leaders, trust between citizens, and trust between institutions.** Corruption erodes that trust, it destroys the very foundation of our society. But when we choose integrity over deceit, when we choose transparency over secrecy, we rebuild that trust.

Imagine an India where trust is the currency of every transaction, where fairness is the norm, and where

justice prevails. This is not a dream—it is a reality we can create if we work together.

Our Call to Action: What Will You Do?

The question now is simple: **What will you do?** Will you continue to accept a system that rewards corruption, or will you rise and be the change you wish to see in India? Will you speak out against bribery when you see it, or will you remain silent? Will you fight for justice, or will you sit back and allow corruption to thrive?

The choice is yours. The future of India rests in your hands. **You have the power to shape the nation you want to see.** And as more and more people rise up, as more and more people decide to take a stand, we will see the change we've been fighting for.

The Strength of Hope

In the darkest moments, it is hope that keeps us going. **Hope is the fire that burns in our hearts, pushing us forward when we feel we can't go on.** Hope is what drives us to speak up, to act, and to believe that change is possible. Without hope, we have nothing.

But with hope, **we have everything. Hope is our most powerful weapon** in the fight against corruption. And as long as we have hope, we will never give up.

A Promise for the Future

We make this promise today: **We will not stop fighting for the India we believe in.** We will not stop until corruption is no longer a part of our lives. We will not stop until we have built a nation based on integrity, fairness, and justice. We will not stop until we leave behind a legacy of truth and transparency.

This is our promise. **We will keep pushing forward, together.**

The Journey Continues

The road ahead is long and filled with challenges. But we do not walk it alone. **We walk it together.** Every step we take is a step toward a brighter, more just India. Every action we take, no matter how small, brings us closer to the country we deserve.

The fight against corruption is not a sprint—it is a marathon. But **we will run this race together**, with strength, with hope, and with the determination to make a difference.

Together, we will build the India we dream of. **Together, we will make it happen.**

Our Future Starts Now

The time to act is now. The future is in our hands. **The future is in your hands.**

Together, we can make India a shining example for the world. **Together, we will create a legacy of hope, justice, and integrity that will inspire generations to come.**

Let's rise together. Let's be the change. Let's build the future of India, today.

The Power of Every Voice

Each voice matters. **Every voice counts.** Even when you feel like your words are too small or too quiet to make a difference, remember that **a single voice can start a revolution.** When we raise our voices in unity, **we create a wave of change** that can ripple across every part of society.

It's not just about shouting the loudest—it's about speaking the truth, standing up for what's right, and refusing to be silenced. **Your voice is your power.** Whether you're standing on the street, in your community, or at a political rally, **your voice is heard**. When millions of voices speak together, they become impossible to ignore.

India's future will be shaped by the voices of its people. And together, we will create a chorus so powerful, it cannot be silenced.

The Call for Accountability

One of the greatest steps toward ending corruption is accountability. **We must hold those in power accountable.** No one, no matter how wealthy or influential, should be above the law. When leaders abuse their positions, they betray the very people who entrusted them with power.

But accountability isn't just for the powerful. **It's for each of us.** Every citizen must be accountable for their actions, for the choices they make. **Integrity starts with us.** If we want to live in a country where corruption no longer thrives, we must first look at ourselves. Are we upholding the values we demand from others? Are we walking the path we want our leaders to follow?

The journey toward a corruption-free India starts with accountability, **and it starts with each and every one of us.**

The Courage to Say No

One of the hardest things to do in a corrupt system is to say **no.** It's easier to give in, to accept the bribe, to look the other way. But courage is not the absence of fear; it's the strength to act despite fear. **Saying no to corruption takes courage.**

It takes courage to stand firm when others are willing to compromise. It takes courage to refuse to be part of a broken system, to challenge those who believe they can buy their way through life. **It takes courage to be the change.**

But here's the thing: **every time we say no to corruption, we empower others to do the same.** The more we stand firm, the more we inspire others to rise. Together, we create a movement that is unstoppable. **We become a force that no one can ignore.**

The Rise of Integrity

Imagine a country where integrity is the norm. **Where honesty and fairness are the pillars that hold us up.** Picture an India where every transaction, every deal, every decision is based on what is right, not what is profitable. **This is the India we can create.**

But to build that India, we must first build a foundation of integrity within ourselves. We must be the living examples of what we want to see in the world. When we act with integrity, we encourage others to do the same. And as more and more people choose integrity over corruption, we will see a ripple effect across the country.

Integrity is the future of India. And it starts with us.

The Courage to Dream Again

Corruption has a way of stealing our dreams. It makes us question whether justice is possible, whether the fight for fairness is even worth it. But **we must dream again.**

We must dream of an India where our children can grow up without having to worry about bribery or favoritism. Where they can aspire to be doctors, teachers, engineers, and leaders, not by paying a price, but by earning their way through merit. **We must dream of a future that is fair, just, and full of opportunity for all.**

And **dreams are not meant to stay dreams**—they are meant to be realized. Every dream of a better India can become a reality if we all work together. **We must dare to dream of a country free from corruption, and then dare to make it happen.**

The Strength of Unity

It is easy to feel alone in the fight against corruption. We may think that our individual efforts are too small to make a difference. But let me remind you: **we are never alone.**

When we stand together, we become unstoppable. **Unity is our strength.** When we come together as one, we create a force so powerful that corruption will have no choice but to crumble before it. **Together, we are invincible.**

Each and every one of us has a role to play in this movement. And when we unite, we become a voice so loud, a force so strong, that no one—no matter how powerful—can stand against us. **Unity is the key to our success.**

The Promise of Change

We have made mistakes. We have faltered. But **we are not defined by our past**. The future is ours to shape. And we must make the promise today that **we will not let corruption continue to destroy our nation**. We will fight for a better India. We will fight for an India built on trust, justice, and fairness.

We owe it to ourselves. We owe it to our children. We owe it to the generations to come.

We will make this promise together, and we will keep it. We will build a future where integrity reigns, where the corrupt are held accountable, and where justice is not a dream, but a reality.

This is our fight. **This is our promise.**

Our Legacy of Hope

As we look toward the future, we have the opportunity to create a legacy that will last for generations. We can be the generation that stands up to corruption. We can be the generation that fights for justice. We can be the generation that makes India a shining example to the world.

This is our moment to leave a legacy of hope, integrity, and justice. **We will be remembered not for the struggles we faced, but for the strength we found in those struggles.** We will be remembered as the generation that chose to rise up and make the world a better place.

The time to act is now. The change we seek begins with us. Let us be the legacy that future generations look to with pride and gratitude.

The End of the Beginning

The journey to a corruption-free India is not an easy one. It will be filled with challenges, setbacks, and obstacles. But it is a journey worth taking, and it is one that we will walk together.

This is not the end of the fight—it is the beginning. **It is the beginning of a new era.** An era where integrity is the foundation of our society, where justice is the guiding light, and where corruption has no place to hide.

Together, we will make this dream a reality. And together, we will create the India we deserve.

Let us rise, together. The future is in our hands. The change starts now.

The Final Call: A Nation Reborn

This is our moment—**the moment India takes its place as a beacon of hope, justice, and fairness in the world.** For too long, we have seen corruption choke the life out of our dreams, our progress, and our potential. But today, we stand at the threshold of a new beginning. **A new India.**

Can you feel it? The winds of change are stirring, stronger than ever before. We have the power, the courage, and the unity to transform this nation. **Together, we will stand tall, not in fear, but in strength and purpose.** Together, we will tear down the walls of corruption and rebuild a nation grounded in truth, fairness, and love for each other.

We will not wait for someone else to lead us. **We will lead ourselves.**

The time has come for every one of us to say, "I will do my part." Whether it's standing up in our communities, speaking out in our workplaces, or demanding accountability from those in power, **our actions will create the world we want to live in.**

This is not just about fighting for today—it's about building a legacy for tomorrow. We must **look into the eyes of our children, our future, and know that we have done everything in our power to give them a better, brighter, and fairer India.**

We Are The Architects of Our Future

We are not powerless. **We are the architects of our own future.** The structures of injustice, greed, and corruption will crumble, brick by brick, as we lay the foundation of integrity, fairness, and accountability. It will not happen overnight, but with each step we take, with each choice we make, we move closer to the India we deserve. **An India where honesty and integrity are not exceptions, but the rule.**

We are not just building a nation—we are building a home, a place where **every citizen feels safe, valued, and empowered.** A home where corruption has no place, where every child's future is filled with promise, and where fairness is the currency that everyone values.

This is our calling. To be the generation that steps up and says, "Enough is enough." We will no longer allow corruption to hold us back. We will fight for a better India because **we are the change we've been waiting for.**

Hope is Our Strength

There will be moments when it feels like we are swimming against the tide, moments when the weight of corruption seems too heavy to bear. But in those moments, **hope will be our strength**. Hope is the fire that burns within us, propelling us forward when the road is tough.

Without hope, we would have nothing to fight for. But with hope, **we can move mountains**. Hope will sustain us when the going gets rough, and it will light our path when we feel lost. Hope will unite us in our common cause and help us see beyond the challenges to the victory that awaits.

We are not fighting alone. **Hope is with us, and together, we will overcome.**

Every Action Counts

It's easy to feel like we are too small to make a real difference, like our voices don't matter in a system so large and so entrenched in corruption. But that's simply not true. **Every action counts.**

Every time we choose honesty over bribery, every time we speak out against injustice, every time we choose integrity over convenience, we are contributing to the change we wish to see in the world. **We are writing the story of a new India with every decision we make.**

Our collective efforts will create a ripple effect that will spread across the nation. **We will inspire others to take action, and together, we will build the country we know is possible.**

The Power of Collective Will

This battle is not one we can fight alone. **It will take all of us, working together, to make the change we want to see.** It will take the courage of every citizen to stand up and speak out. It will take the power of the people to hold those in power accountable. And it will take the commitment of every individual to choose integrity over corruption.

But together, we are unstoppable. **Together, we can change the course of our nation.**

The strength of a country lies in its people. **When the people unite, nothing can stand in their way.** And we, the people of India, are united in our desire to create a country that is just, fair, and free from corruption.

A New Dawn for India

Look around you, and you will see signs of change everywhere. The movement is growing. More and more people are beginning to speak out. More and more voices are rising, demanding change. **This is the beginning of a new dawn for India.**

The old ways of corruption, deceit, and bribery are crumbling, and in their place, **a new India is emerging**—a country founded on integrity, fairness, and accountability. It will take time, but we are moving in the right direction.

The road ahead will not always be easy, but **we will walk it together.** We will be there for each other, supporting one another as we fight for the future of this great nation.

The Fight Continues—But We Are Not Alone

Even as we face obstacles, even as we encounter setbacks, let us remember this: **We are not alone in this fight.**

We are standing shoulder to shoulder with millions of other Indians who are tired of the corruption, tired of the bribery, tired of the injustice. Together, we are a force that cannot be defeated. **We will keep pushing forward, and we will win.**

This fight is not just for us—it's for our children, for the future generations of Indians who deserve a better life. It's for the farmers, the teachers, the workers, the doctors, the students—**it's for every single person who believes in the power of honesty, the power of truth, and the power of change.**

Conclusion: Our Time Has Come

The time for change is now. **We stand at the crossroads of history**, and the decisions we make today will shape the future of India for generations to come.

This is our call to action. **We must rise up and make our voices heard.** We must stand up against corruption, against injustice, and against the forces that seek to hold us back. Together, we will create an India that is worthy of our dreams.

We will build an India where integrity is the foundation, where justice is the standard, and where fairness is the rule.

The fight is not over. The fight has just begun. And together, we will win.

Let us rise, united in our cause, with hope in our hearts, and strength in our voices. Together, we will create the India we know is possible.

The Strength in Our Struggles

Our journey has not been without pain. **We have been wounded by corruption**, scarred by its relentless grip on every part of our lives. But it's in our struggles that we find our true strength. The road has been hard, the obstacles have been many, but **we have never stopped moving forward.**

Every setback is a lesson. Every challenge is an opportunity to grow stronger, to rise higher, and to prove that we will not be defeated. Yes, corruption has caused suffering, but it has also birthed a new spirit in us—a spirit of resistance, resilience, and hope.

We are more than the sum of our struggles. We are the living proof that, no matter how deep the corruption runs, the people's will can always rise above it. **Our strength lies in our ability to endure**, to continue fighting even when it feels like the world is against us.

The Vision for Tomorrow

What does the future of India look like? **It is a vision of fairness.** A vision where the law applies equally to all, regardless of their wealth, power, or status. It is a vision where justice is not a privilege but a right, where integrity is the foundation of every institution, and where every citizen, regardless of their background, can walk with their heads held high.

But it's more than just a dream—it's a **vision we will bring to life**. Through our actions, our courage, and our unshakable belief in what is right, we will turn this vision into reality. We will no longer stand by as corruption tarnishes our society. **We will rise up together** to build the India we know is possible.

This is our promise: **A future where corruption has no place. A future where justice prevails.**

Embracing the Challenge

The challenge before us is monumental, but so is our capacity to face it. It will take every ounce of courage, every drop of sweat, every voice raised in protest. But we can do it. **We can face the challenge of corruption and overcome it.**

Yes, there will be days when we feel exhausted, when the weight of the battle feels too much to bear. **But we must remember: we are not fighting this alone.** We are a nation united in purpose, driven by the collective will of the people who believe in a better tomorrow.

So let us embrace this challenge, for **it is in facing the hardest of trials that we discover our deepest strength.** Together, we will rise to meet it and emerge victorious.

The Heartbeat of Change

There is a heartbeat that echoes through India—a heartbeat of change. **It is the pulse of the people who are tired of injustice and eager to create a new future.** We are the heartbeat of a nation on the brink of transformation, ready to rewrite its story and reclaim its destiny.

Every step we take brings us closer to the India we envision. Every small act of defiance against corruption, every moment of standing up for what is right, contributes to the collective momentum of change.

We are the heart of this movement. And as long as our hearts beat, as long as we stand together in solidarity, there is nothing that can stop us.

The Courage to Dream Big

In times of corruption, it's easy to feel small, to feel like our dreams are out of reach. But let us remember this: **we must dare to dream big.** Our dreams are what fuel our passion, our drive, and our actions. And the bigger the dream, the more powerful the movement.

We dream of an India where corruption is a thing of the past. We dream of a society where equality reigns, where justice is blind to wealth and power. **We dream of an India that stands tall on the global stage, not just for its strength, but for its integrity.**

And these are not just dreams. **They are the blueprints for our future.** Together, we will make them a reality.

The Unbreakable Bond of Unity

India's strength has always been its people. **When we stand united, we are unstoppable.** The power of a united India cannot be measured—it can only be felt.

Corruption has tried to divide us, to pit us against one another, but **we will not let it succeed.** Our diversity is our greatest strength. Our different languages, cultures, and religions are not barriers but bridges to understanding, compassion, and unity. Together, we are a force so powerful that it cannot be ignored.

When we unite, we become the change we seek. No corrupt system, no powerful individual, can withstand the strength of a united nation determined to create a future free of corruption.

The Resilience to Never Give Up

The fight against corruption is not for the faint-hearted. It is a long and often difficult battle. There will be moments when it feels like we are moving forward only to be pushed two steps back. But it is in these moments of struggle that our **resilience will shine brightest.**

We will not give up. **We will never stop fighting.** With every challenge, our resolve grows stronger. With every setback, our spirit becomes more unbreakable.

This is not just a battle for today—it's a battle for the future. **A future where our children and grandchildren can live in a country that values integrity, equality, and justice.**

So, let us stand firm. **Let us refuse to back down.** Let us show the world that the people of India are unstoppable when they fight for what is right.

A Future Without Fear

Corruption instills fear—fear of retribution, fear of being silenced, fear of standing up for what's right. But in this new India, we will live **without fear**. We will no longer be afraid to speak the truth, to demand justice, or to stand up against those who try to buy their way through life.

The fear that once held us back will be replaced by the courage that propels us forward. We will no longer cower in the shadows of corruption—we will stand proudly in the light of a new India. A nation where the people are not afraid of the system, but the system is afraid of the people.

The Promise of a Just Future

As we stand on the precipice of this new era, we must make one promise—**to never forget why we fight.** We fight for justice. We fight for the voiceless. We fight for the future of our children.

We fight for a country where corruption no longer defines us. Where the corrupt no longer thrive in the shadows of power. **We fight for a nation that reflects the values we hold dear—honesty, fairness, and equality for all.**

This is not just a battle—it is a promise. **A promise that we will keep.** We will build a future where corruption is no longer tolerated, where justice is not delayed, and where every citizen is free to live their life with dignity and respect.

Conclusion: The Dawn of a New India

We are the dreamers, the believers, the fighters, and the changemakers. **We are the dawn of a new India**, and together, we will make that dawn brighter than any we have ever known.

We will not wait for change. **We will create it.**

And when the history books are written, they will speak of a nation that stood up, a nation that fought back, and a nation that triumphed over corruption. This is our story—and together, we will make it legendary.

The future of India is in our hands. The time for change is now. Let's rise, united in purpose and vision, and build the India we've always dreamed of.

The fight continues, the hope remains, and together, we will rise.

The Heart of the Nation: The People's Will

It is said that the heart of a nation beats in the hearts of its people. **India's heartbeat is strong**, pulsing with the desires of millions who refuse to be silenced by corruption. We are a people of immense courage, resilience, and determination. **The power of our collective will is unstoppable.**

Every single person who dares to stand up against the system, who speaks out in the face of fear, who refuses to be cowed by the weight of corruption, is part of this collective force. **Our unity is our strength**, and as long as we remain united in our vision for a fairer, just India, no force in the world can break us.

Let's take a moment to reflect—**what would our country look like if every citizen stood firm in their belief that change is possible?** What if every person took one small step toward dismantling the system of corruption, refusing to participate, and demanding a better future? **The answer is clear:** we would be unstoppable.

India's future is built not on the whims of the powerful, but on the shoulders of its people. **Together, we are the engine of change, the driving force behind the transformation of our nation.**

Fighting for Every Voice

Throughout history, it has often been the quiet voices that have sparked the greatest revolutions. **It is the voices of the marginalized, the oppressed, and the forgotten that have ignited the flames of justice.** In the fight against corruption, we must honor every voice that has been silenced by fear, every person who has suffered in silence because they believed their cries would never be heard.

Our fight is for every single person in India who has been crushed under the weight of injustice. It is for the farmer who struggles to make ends meet, the teacher who works tirelessly for little reward, the woman who is denied equal rights, and the child who dreams of a future free from corruption and poverty. **We fight for the dreamers, the workers, the parents, and the leaders of tomorrow.**

The time has come for every voice to rise. **When the people speak together, nothing can stop them.**

The Courage to Challenge the Status Quo

Challenging the status quo is never easy. It takes immense courage to stand up against a system that is deeply entrenched, to fight against those who have grown accustomed to the power that corruption affords them. But the truth is simple: **courage is not the absence of fear—it is the willingness to act despite it.**

We must be the generation that **dares to challenge the powerful**, that stands up and says, "We will no longer allow corruption to dictate our lives." We must not shrink in the face of adversity. **Instead, we must rise, boldly and without hesitation**, because every step we take brings us closer to a future where justice and fairness prevail.

Yes, the road is long. Yes, the challenges are great. But the courage of the people of India is even greater. **And when courage leads the way, nothing is impossible.**

The Power of Transparency

At the heart of any corrupt system is a lack of transparency. **Corruption thrives in the shadows**, where actions are hidden from public view, and accountability is elusive. But transparency is a weapon. **When we expose the truth, when we shine a light on the dark corners where corruption hides, we take away its power.**

We must demand transparency in every facet of life—in government, in business, in our everyday interactions. **We must insist on knowing how decisions are made, who is benefiting from them, and who is being left behind.**

It is only through transparency that we can create an environment where corruption has nowhere to hide. **It is only through transparency that we can build a system where the truth prevails and justice is served.**

The Flame of Hope Will Never Die

In every generation, there comes a time when people must decide whether they will accept the world as it is or fight to change it. **We are at that crossroads now.** We can no longer afford to sit on the sidelines and hope for change. **The time for hope without action is over.**

But here's the thing: **hope is not passive.** Hope is what drives us to act. It is the spark that ignites a movement, that lights the way even when the path seems unclear. **Hope is our greatest weapon**—and as long as we hold onto it, we will never lose the fight against corruption.

Hope is what keeps us going when the days are long and the obstacles are high. **It is what gives us the strength to rise**

again, no matter how many times we fall. Hope is the fuel that keeps our hearts burning, even when the fire seems to flicker.

And as long as that flame burns in our hearts, we will not stop. **We will keep fighting, we will keep pushing, and we will keep hoping**—because we know that hope will one day turn into victory.

Our Legacy: A Gift to Future Generations

What will we leave behind? **The choices we make today will shape the India of tomorrow.** The values we instill, the actions we take, the stand we make against corruption will create a legacy that will echo through generations.

Our children deserve more than just empty promises. **They deserve an India where they can live free from fear, where they can walk the streets knowing that justice is on their side.** They deserve an India where corruption is not the norm, but the exception. **They deserve an India where integrity is celebrated, and honesty is rewarded.**

This fight is not just for us. **It is for those who come after us.** We must create a nation worthy of their dreams, a country where they will never have to fight the battles we fought. **Our legacy will be a nation of justice, of fairness, and of unshakable integrity.**

A Nation Reborn

When we look around us today, it may seem like nothing has changed. But don't be fooled. **The seeds of transformation have already been planted.** They are growing, quietly but steadily, in the hearts of every citizen who refuses to accept corruption as the status quo. **A new India is already being born.**

It is being born in the courage of every protester who stands in the streets, in the bravery of every whistleblower who exposes wrongdoing, in the integrity of every public servant who chooses honesty over greed. **It is being born in the hearts of millions who dare to dream of a better future.**

And while the battle is far from over, we can say this with certainty: **The future of India is bright, and the dawn of a new era is on the horizon.**

Conclusion: Together, We Rise

The journey ahead will not be easy. But one thing is certain: **We will rise together.** We will rise as a united nation, bound by a common cause, driven by a common purpose, and filled with an unbreakable will to create a better India.

We will rise, not in fear, but in strength. **We will rise, not in doubt, but in hope.** We will rise, and with every rise, we will take one more step toward the India we know is possible.

So, let us stand together, shoulder to shoulder, **and fight for the India we deserve.** Our time has come. The time for change is now. **And together, we will make that change happen.**

India, we rise.

With hope in our hearts and determination in our souls, we will create the India of our dreams.

Chapter-15

How America Dominates the World with Money and Divide-and-Rule Tactics: India's Smart Strategy in the Global Game

The United States has long held a position of power in the world, not just through military might but also through a subtle yet powerful tool—its money diplomacy. From shaping global markets to influencing political decisions, America's ability to wield its wealth has been at the heart of its strategy for decades. However, what many don't see is how this dominance is not just about strength, but about a shrewd use of resources to divide nations, manipulate economies, and control the global narrative.

The Power of Money Diplomacy

Money, as they say, makes the world go round. And no one understands this better than the United States. Through institutions like the World Bank and the International Monetary Fund (IMF), the U.S. has crafted a system that forces poorer nations into debt traps. By offering loans to struggling countries, often with conditions that limit their sovereignty, America has turned these financial institutions into tools of influence.

But it doesn’t stop there. The U.S. dollar is the world's primary trade currency, and this is where America's true dominance lies. Nations must hold dollars to trade, invest, and do business globally. This dependency on the U.S. dollar gives America unparalleled leverage. When America sneezes, the whole world catches a cold. Just one change in U.S. monetary policy can send shockwaves across the globe, affecting everything from oil prices to food costs in the most remote villages.

Divide and Rule: America's Subtle Tactics

Beyond economic control, the U.S. has perfected a technique of "divide and rule" that has kept its power intact for generations. It’s not enough for America to simply dominate; it has worked tirelessly to create divisions between countries, sowing distrust, and creating conflicts that serve its own interests.

Take the example of global alliances. The U.S. often forms strategic partnerships based on economic or military interests, but these alliances come with strings attached. America encourages tensions between nations, often exploiting existing rivalries, so that countries remain reliant on the U.S. for security, trade, and aid. By doing so, it ensures that no one nation becomes strong enough to challenge its supremacy.

India’s Strategic Game: A Rising Power

In this complex web of global politics, India has emerged as a nation that is playing its cards smartly. While the U.S. has historically been seen as the world's policeman, India is positioning itself as a key player in the new world order. But how?

India has recognized the importance of maintaining strong relations with the United States, not just as a global power, but as an economic powerhouse. However, India isn't blindly following America's lead. It is, instead, forging its own path by balancing its alliances carefully. While it embraces the benefits of a relationship with the U.S., it is also building strategic ties with other global players like Russia, China, and countries in the Middle East.

India's growing economic influence, technological advancements, and military might have placed it in a unique position. India's relationship with the U.S. is one of mutual respect, not subservience. India understands that the U.S. is a powerful partner, but it also knows that it cannot afford to be too dependent. The key to India's smart diplomacy is understanding when to play along and when to push back.

Playing the Game Smartly: India's Calculated Approach

India's foreign policy has evolved. Unlike many smaller nations, which feel pressured to align with U.S. policies, India knows the importance of playing the game with intelligence. India seeks to build alliances that benefit its people and its economy, ensuring that it remains strong on its own terms.

Take, for instance, India's neutral stance in the U.S.-China trade war. While many countries had to take sides, India capitalized on the opportunity to boost its own manufacturing sector. It attracted companies looking to move out of China due to trade tensions. By positioning itself as a hub for global manufacturing, India enhanced its own economic growth while avoiding getting entangled in global conflicts that don't serve its interests.

At the same time, India has maintained strong relationships with key players in the world, including Russia, Europe, and countries in Africa and the Middle East. By diversifying its alliances, India has created a safety net that keeps it from becoming too reliant on any one power.

Conclusion: The Future of Global Power Dynamics

The United States may dominate the world through its financial influence and divide-and-rule tactics, but nations like India are showing the world how to navigate these power dynamics with wisdom and caution. India's rise on the global stage is not just a result of economic growth, but of a carefully calculated foreign policy strategy that refuses to be dictated by any single power.

As the world shifts toward a multipolar future, India's smart diplomacy will serve as a model for other nations seeking to maintain their sovereignty while navigating the complexities of global politics. The U.S. may have its dollar, but India's strategy is based on something far more powerful—independence, intelligence, and the strength of a people who know how to play the game on their own terms.

In a world ruled by money and power, India is proving that you don't have to be the richest or the most powerful to win. You just have to be smart enough to play the game the right way.

A Nation That Thinks for Itself

What makes India's strategy so remarkable is that it is not bound by historical dependencies or old alliances. It does not blindly follow the commands of global superpowers, nor does it bend under the pressure of foreign influence. India, with its rich cultural heritage and diverse society, has always been a land that prided itself on its independence. This spirit of independence is reflected in its foreign policy—an approach that champions diplomacy, mutual respect, and strength through diversity.

In the face of U.S. economic dominance, India has charted its own path, setting an example for other nations. While the United States may use its money as a tool to secure loyalty, India understands that true strength lies in the ability to stand tall, without compromising its values or sovereignty. India has risen, not because it followed the U.S. blindly, but because it chose to walk alongside it as an equal partner, playing the long game with patience, strategy, and foresight.

A New World Order: India's Role in Shaping the Future

As we look toward the future, it's clear that the world is changing. The U.S. may still wield significant influence, but its grip on the global stage is beginning to loosen. The rise of new powers, like China and India, is challenging the old world order, and this is something the U.S. cannot ignore.

What we are witnessing is not just a shift in economic power, but a shift in the way nations view their role in the world. The U.S. may have once used divide-and-rule tactics to keep countries in line, but now, countries like India are learning to leverage their strengths, form new alliances, and control their own destiny. The balance of power is no longer solely in the hands of the West. It is being redefined by emerging nations that understand the value of collaboration, diplomacy, and mutual benefit.

India's relationship with the U.S. will continue to be vital, but it is no longer the only axis around which the world turns. India's ability to maintain independence while working with multiple partners in a complex global environment shows that the future will be one of strategic cooperation, not domination.

A Call for Unity and Change

In the end, what is the real lesson here? It is not just about the rise of one nation over another. It is about the realization that no country should have to live under the shadow of another. The U.S. may have perfected the art of economic influence and political maneuvering, but it is the rise of nations like India that offer hope for a world where countries have the freedom to choose their path without fear of outside interference.

For India, the message is clear: the road to success lies in smart diplomacy, in building strong relationships, and in protecting what makes a nation unique. India's rise is not just an economic miracle—it is a triumph of willpower, intelligence, and resilience. It is proof that even in a world dominated by money and power, the human spirit can carve out its own space and make its voice heard.

This is a call to all nations, big and small: Stand strong. Work smart. Know that you have the power to shape your own future. The game is no longer just about following the rules set by others; it's about creating your own. And India is leading the way, showing the world that with courage, vision, and unity, anything is possible.

Empire of Influence: How the United States Shapes Global Corruption and Power"

Fact 1: The Foundations of Global Corruption

- **Overview of Corruption as a Tool of Control**
  - Definition and types of corruption; how corruption pervades economies globally.
  - Historical look at how powerful nations use corruption to keep other nations dependent.
- **Case Studies of Economic Manipulation**
  - Examples of U.S. interventions in economically vulnerable nations (Latin America, the Middle East).
  - Analysis of U.S. policies that keep weaker nations dependent (e.g., foreign aid with strings attached, conditional loans, and favorable trade deals).

Fact 2: Dollar Dominance and the Weakening of World Currencies

- **Rise of the Dollar as a World Reserve Currency**
  - Explanation of the Bretton Woods agreement, petrodollars, and the dollar's global role.
  - Impact on other currencies: how pegging to the dollar keeps weaker economies from growing independently.

- **How Dollar Dependence Drives Global Inequality**
  - Insight into currency devaluation in other countries due to dollar-centric policies.
  - Real-world impact on developing nations, including inflation, debt traps, and reduced local buying power.

Fact 3: Division by Design: The U.S. Role in Disunity

- **The Geopolitical Strategy of Divide and Conquer**
  - How the U.S. uses internal divisions within countries to its advantage (e.g., supporting opposition groups).
  - Economic sanctions and the U.S.'s role in destabilizing governments that oppose its interests.
- **Influence on Social Movements and Political Crises**
  - U.S. involvement in political movements globally (Arab Spring, Eastern Europe).
  - Strategies to keep foreign powers disunited, making it easier to dominate economically and politically.

Fact 4: The Billionaire Effect: Wealth, Politics, and Power in the U.S.

- **Billionaire Influence on U.S. Elections and Policy**
    - Overview of campaign finance, lobbying, and the Citizens United ruling.
    - How billionaires secure political influence, influencing everything from domestic policy to foreign aid and trade.
- **Implications for Global Corruption and Economic Control**
    - How billionaire interests shape U.S. foreign policy and economic strategies.
    - Closing thoughts on how the intertwining of money, politics, and corruption in the U.S. impacts global stability and fairness.

Corruption is everywhere, but in India, it can often feel like a part of daily life. From the chai-paani (a term commonly used for small bribes) to larger-scale scams that make headlines, the common man is caught in a system that demands shortcuts. This book will explore how corruption and bribery seep into our lives, often in ways we may not even realize. Through real-life examples and relatable scenarios, we'll explore how this problem persists and what we, as everyday citizens, face.

The Price of a Simple Signature

Have you ever tried to get a simple government document like a driving license or a ration card? The process can take days, even months—unless you "speed things up" with some extra cash. This section dives into everyday examples of how corruption makes simple tasks complicated. From bribing government officials to get a faster passport to paying off clerks for school admissions, every level of society feels the pinch. It shows how the common person is forced into situations where paying a bribe feels like the only option to get things done.

The Corruption in Public Services

Public services like health, police, and education are supposed to serve the people, but often they become sources of harassment and delay without a "fee" to grease the wheels. This section looks at stories of people in small towns and cities who have had to bribe their way into hospitals, police stations, or even schools. These are real-life situations where the need for basic services becomes a game of money, and how this affects the poorer sections of society the most.

Bribery in Elections: Buying Votes, Losing Hope

Corruption doesn't just exist in government offices—it's deeply rooted in our democracy. During elections, candidates distribute cash, alcohol, and other items to buy votes, making elections a mockery of democracy. This section explores how people in different parts of India witness this vote-buying culture, where promises are made, money is exchanged, and after the elections, nothing changes. It explains how these practices erode faith in the system and leave the common man feeling cheated.

Corporate Corruption: When Big Money Changes Hands

It's not just the public sector—private companies, too, are knee-deep in corruption. Whether it's large corporations bribing officials to get favorable contracts or small businesses paying to avoid harassment from tax authorities, this section explains how corruption at the corporate level trickles down. The story of a businessman who refuses to pay a bribe, and what happens to him and his business, sheds light on how corruption in big business affects everyday lives.

The Web of Middlemen

Middlemen—those who help "get the work done" for a price—are a common feature in Indian bureaucracy. They are the unofficial bridge between citizens and officials. This section covers stories of how middlemen operate in various sectors like real estate, government offices, and courts. By relying on middlemen, the system itself has become corrupt, and this chapter highlights how people often don't know where to turn when every door seems closed without "help."

Scams That Shock the Nation

India has witnessed several major scams in its history, from the 2G spectrum scandal to the coal allocation scam. While these scams involve mind-boggling amounts of money, the real victims are ordinary people who lose access to resources that are meant for public good. This chapter briefly examines these scams and connects them to the daily struggles of common people, showing how the big players in corruption affect even the smallest corners of the country.

The Burden on the Poor

For the wealthy, paying a bribe might just be a way to avoid hassles. But for the poor, it can be a devastating burden. Imagine a daily wage laborer paying off officials to get government benefits meant for his family. This section examines how corruption widens the gap between the rich and poor and makes it even harder for those at the bottom to rise. Personal stories of individuals in rural India paint a vivid picture of the struggles they face.

Solutions: Can We Fight Corruption?

While it may feel like corruption is unbeatable, there are efforts at many levels to fight it. From stronger laws to citizen activism, this final section highlights small but significant victories against corruption. It also touches on how technology, like digital payments and online government services, is reducing the scope for bribery. Ultimately, this book asks the reader: Can we, as citizens, be the change we want to see? How can we refuse to participate in this system and build a more transparent, fair society?

Conclusion:

Corruption in India is not just a political issue; it's a personal one. It affects us in our daily lives, and unless we acknowledge it, we cannot fight it. This book is a reminder that change is possible—but only if we are willing to take that first step.

The Promise of Tomorrow

As the sun rises over India, there is an undeniable sense of hope. Hope for a world where no nation is left behind. Hope for a world where every country has the ability to thrive, to build its own future, and to play a role in shaping the global story. India's journey is far from over, but one thing is certain: it will no longer be content to play in the background.

India is not just a rising power. It is the future. And the world, for all its divisions, will have to reckon with the strength, the ambition, and the wisdom that this great nation brings to the table.

So, as the global balance of power shifts, let us watch closely. Let us witness how India, through its intelligence, its diplomacy, and its unwavering commitment to its people, stands as a shining example for the rest of the world. A new world is on the horizon—a world where the old rules no longer apply, and where the nations that dare to dream and stand tall will shape the future. India is leading the charge, and its story is one we will all remember.

Chapter-16

Corruption in Top Hospitals: Pre and Post COVID-19 Effect

Before COVID-19, corruption was already present in the healthcare system, but the pandemic took it to new heights. The crisis revealed the profit-driven motives of many top hospitals, especially during the second wave, when millions of families in India were desperate for care.

In April 2021, I admitted my father to a major hospital in Gurugram, Haryana, during the height of the pandemic's second wave. Back then, the hospital's cafeteria was decent—what you'd expect from a good hospital. But when I returned to the same hospital in May 2023, the transformation was shocking. The interiors were completely revamped, and the cafeteria looked more like a five-star hotel lounge. It was hard not to wonder where all this money came from. I could only imagine the profits they must have made during the pandemic to afford such a luxurious renovation in just two years.

During COVID-19, the government urged large hospitals to reduce their charges and serve patients without seeing the crisis as a business opportunity. The government stressed that hospitals should not exploit patients during such a critical time. But those appeals went ignored, as many hospitals treated the pandemic as a chance to make unprecedented profits, charging exorbitant fees that families struggled to pay. If hospitals refused to listen even to the government's appeal, what chance did ordinary people like us stand? It felt utterly helpless. All the major multi-specialty hospitals in the Delhi-Gurgaon area were renovated as if they were luxury hotels. And these hospitals even had bouncers—a chilling sight in a place meant for healing and care. Imagine that: hospitals with bouncers! If a patient's family didn't comply with their rules, raised concerns about the high costs, or couldn't pay, they would be thrown out.

This isn't something you can find on Google. I saw it with my own eyes, especially in 2021, when I lost my father in the very same hospital. This is the dark reality of the healthcare system in India. While I don't hold the doctors entirely responsible, I cannot ignore the hospital management's role in this unchecked greed. Doctors, in many ways, are just puppets in the hands of powerful hospital administrators, carrying out whatever they are instructed to do. It's the management that decides policies, pricing, and the extent of care provided to patients, often prioritizing profits over genuine care.

This pandemic, for many, exposed the grim truth about healthcare in India, revealing a system that, for some, put money over lives when people were at their most vulnerable.

The reality of these hospitals was exposed during the pandemic, but the changes go deeper than what's visible. During COVID-19, private hospitals often became profit-driven machines, exploiting patients who had no choice but to pay whatever was asked. Families were desperate, and hospitals leveraged that desperation, knowing that people would do anything to save their loved ones.

The Rising Costs and Unnecessary Charges

It wasn't just about high fees; the billing practices themselves were often designed to drain families financially. Hospitals started imposing charges for everything—oxygen, PPE kits, even extra fees for ICU beds during a time when demand was overwhelming. Simple treatments came with a hefty price tag. Hospitals took advantage of the fact that patients were too overwhelmed or too emotionally invested to question every detail. For example, a simple treatment that would have been affordable pre-COVID suddenly came with inflated charges for "safety protocols," "sanitation fees," and mandatory "special care packages."

Families were billed for multiple unnecessary tests, additional "consultations," and medications they later realized were not even relevant to the patient's condition. It became a common story during the pandemic to hear of bills that left families nearly bankrupt.

Personal Impact: Losing a Loved One and Facing the System's Exploitation

Losing my father in May 2021 made me painfully aware of the realities of healthcare corruption. The bills we received were astronomical, and despite our pleas, the hospital's management showed no empathy or flexibility. After paying everything we could, we still left the hospital with a deep feeling of betrayal, knowing that our loss was treated as just another transaction by the hospital administration. This experience is not just mine—thousands of families across the country faced similar horrors, losing both their loved ones and their financial stability to hospital bills they could hardly afford.

From Healers to Enforcers: When Hospitals Hire Bouncers

When I returned to the hospital in 2023, I saw bouncers stationed in the halls and at every major exit. These security personnel were intimidating, ensuring that anyone who didn't follow the hospital's rules would be immediately removed. Patients' families who couldn't afford the fees were treated not as people in need but as rule-breakers. Hospital management was enforcing their rules as if the hospital was a business establishment where any disturbance to their policies would be met with force.

Hospitals, once considered sanctuaries of healing, have become more like businesses—cold, calculating, and profit-driven. Security guards and bouncers are there to remind families that they are at the mercy of the hospital, where the priority is not care but revenue. If you can't pay, you can't stay. This ruthless approach leaves people helpless, breaking their spirit when they're already vulnerable.

Doctors: Caught Between Duty and Management Pressure

One may assume that doctors, with their dedication to healing, would act against this exploitation. But in these large, private hospitals, doctors are often powerless to challenge management. Many doctors feel pressured to follow instructions, prioritize certain high-cost treatments, or even push unnecessary tests to meet the hospital's financial goals. Their medical expertise is often compromised by management directives focused on increasing revenue.

Doctors, many of whom enter the profession to help others, find themselves entangled in a system where management dictates their actions. They're forced to act as per hospital policies, which are often designed to maximize income. This robs doctors of their autonomy and leaves patients and their families suffering the consequences of a corrupted system that places profit over genuine medical ethics.

Government Appeals and the Failure of Regulation

Throughout the pandemic, the government repeatedly asked hospitals to cap their fees and provide fair treatment options. However, these requests were largely ignored. The healthcare sector, especially private hospitals, continued to charge whatever they wanted, unchecked by any regulatory oversight.

The government's appeals fell on deaf ears, highlighting a critical flaw in the regulatory system. The authorities were unable to enforce price controls effectively or ensure fair practices. This lack of regulation not only enabled hospitals to exploit patients but also allowed them to operate with complete disregard for ethical standards. The absence of strong legal repercussions left hospitals free to pursue profits without accountability, exploiting every loophole in the healthcare system to their advantage.

Hospitals Redesigned as Luxury Hotels: A Testament to Profit

Walking into a hospital that feels like a five-star hotel is jarring, especially when you know the money for this luxury came from patients' pockets. Hospitals in Delhi-Gurgaon have become lavish, with interiors resembling high-end establishments. From luxurious waiting rooms to upgraded private rooms that look like suites, everything screams of money and class. These renovations, though impressive, represent how much the healthcare system has turned into a money-making industry.

While patients might appreciate comfort, the stark contrast between the luxury provided for paying clients and the critical care needed for others underscores the system's skewed priorities. People don't go to hospitals for luxury; they go for life-saving treatment. Yet, hospitals today are prioritizing these upgrades to attract the wealthy, while middle-class families struggle to afford even basic care.

Conclusion: A Call for Accountability in Healthcare

The healthcare system, especially in India's big private hospitals, urgently needs reform. The pandemic exposed the true colors of many hospitals, showing how profit took precedence over people's lives. The system is failing those who need it most, and without changes, it will continue to exploit the very people it is supposed to serve. We need transparency, accountability, and strict regulation to ensure that healthcare remains a fundamental right, not a privilege for those who can afford it.

To truly heal, the system must change. Hospitals should be held accountable, and practices that exploit patients for profit should be met with firm consequences. For families like mine and countless others, who have experienced both loss and financial ruin at the hands of these hospitals, it's crucial that we speak up, demand justice, and push for a system that genuinely cares for its people.

FAQs

1. **How did hospitals exploit patients during the COVID-19 pandemic?**: During COVID-19, many hospitals inflated prices for treatments, ICU beds, oxygen, and even basic equipment, leaving families with overwhelming bills.
2. **Why do some hospitals have bouncers?**: Bouncers in hospitals are often present to enforce hospital policies, ensuring that only compliant patients and families remain, especially regarding payments.
3. **Are doctors to blame for the corruption in hospitals?**: Many doctors are caught between their duty to care for patients and the demands of hospital management, which often prioritizes profit.
4. **What is the government doing to regulate healthcare prices?**: While the government made appeals for price caps during COVID-19, enforcement has been weak, and many private hospitals still operate without strict price regulation.
5. **How can we push for changes in India's healthcare system?**: Public awareness, stronger regulations, and holding hospitals accountable are key

steps in ensuring that healthcare is fair and accessible to all.

Why Healthcare in India Needs Urgent Reform

The COVID-19 pandemic served as a wake-up call, exposing the deep-rooted flaws in India's healthcare system. The government appeals for hospitals to cap prices and provide fair, essential services went mostly unheeded, as financial incentives outweighed ethical responsibilities. The healthcare industry, especially the private sector, showed how unregulated pricing and unchecked power can harm ordinary citizens. Without intervention, these practices will persist, leaving the most vulnerable at risk.

The Power Imbalance: Patients vs. Healthcare Corporations

At the core of this issue is a profound power imbalance. Patients and their families, often emotionally and financially vulnerable, are in no position to negotiate with large, profit-driven hospital chains. They are forced to accept the prices and conditions set by these corporations, without any assurance of fairness. The rise of large hospital chains and networks has made healthcare increasingly monopolized, further limiting patients' choices. For example, when a critical care patient is admitted, families have no time to compare hospitals, which lets hospitals dictate terms knowing the family is desperate for immediate care.

Mental Toll on Families: Navigating a System Built on Profit

The emotional toll of these experiences is hard to quantify but immensely damaging. Families dealing with critical care situations often find themselves exhausted, not just physically and emotionally but financially as well. When a loved one is in the ICU, families don't have the time or mental energy to dispute bills, question unnecessary tests, or challenge aggressive pricing. The system is set up in a way that exploits this vulnerability, knowing that families in distress will pay whatever is necessary, even if it means taking out loans or selling assets.

This is where hospitals have a responsibility to show compassion and integrity. However, when profit becomes the primary goal, compassion takes a back seat. Instead of supporting patients, the current system makes an already heartbreaking situation even worse by piling financial stress onto emotional suffering. In the end, families are left with an immense burden, facing a lifetime of debt or financial instability due to inflated healthcare costs.

The Role of Regulatory Bodies: Where Are the Enforcements?

In theory, regulatory bodies like the Medical Council of India (MCI) and National Accreditation Board for Hospitals & Healthcare Providers (NABH) are responsible for ensuring ethical practices. However, the lack of strong enforcement has allowed these issues to spiral out of control. Inspections and audits need to be frequent, transparent, and conducted by independent parties to ensure there are no conflicts of interest. Additionally, these regulatory bodies need to take proactive measures, such as imposing penalties on hospitals found guilty of unfair pricing, unethical practices, or failure to comply with government guidelines.

Regulations on healthcare costs and services should be introduced at a national level. Having clear, legally enforced guidelines can prevent hospitals from manipulating prices or providing unnecessary services just to inflate bills. This type of oversight is critical, especially during crises, to prevent healthcare providers from capitalizing on people's vulnerabilities.

A Roadmap for Change: What Needs to Be Done

To rebuild public trust in healthcare, the following actions should be prioritized:

1. **Enforce Transparent Pricing:** All hospitals should be required to publish a standardized rate card, outlining the costs of essential treatments, diagnostics, and services. Any deviation should be justified and made publicly available.

2. **Cap Fees for Essential Services:** The government should set a ceiling on charges for essential services, especially during emergencies like pandemics, ensuring hospitals cannot exploit patients in desperate situations.

3. **Mandatory Audits and Penalties:** Independent, frequent audits should be mandatory, with strict penalties for hospitals caught inflating prices or conducting unnecessary tests solely for profit.

4. **Patient Rights Awareness Campaigns:** Patients and families need to be aware of their rights within the healthcare system. A national campaign can educate the public about fair billing practices, complaint processes, and ways to report unethical behavior.

5. **Support Systems for Low-Income Families:** Healthcare costs can financially devastate families, especially those with limited resources. The government should enhance healthcare subsidies, expand access to

affordable insurance, and develop schemes to support low-income families facing medical emergencies.

Fighting for Accountability: How the Public Can Play a Role

Raising public awareness is one of the most effective ways to drive change. With access to information, people can demand more transparency and accountability from healthcare providers. Social media and digital platforms can be powerful tools for patients to share their stories, exposing unethical practices and putting pressure on hospitals to reform. By coming together, patients and families can amplify their voices and create a groundswell of demand for change.

Furthermore, legal action is an option, albeit a challenging one. Patients who have faced exploitation can come together to form class-action lawsuits against hospitals that have consistently engaged in predatory practices. While this approach requires resources, it's a powerful way to hold hospitals accountable and send a clear message that exploitation will not be tolerated.

Building a Compassionate, Patient-Centered Healthcare System

The ideal healthcare system prioritizes patients' well-being over profits. A patient-centered system should uphold compassion, transparency, and fairness as its core values. Healthcare facilities should not be seen as money-making enterprises but as places of healing and support.

In the future, we should aim for a system where hospitals don't just treat patients but actively support their financial and emotional well-being. Medical costs should not come as a devastating shock but be managed fairly, with an understanding that people's lives are at stake. A compassionate healthcare system respects each patient and their family, recognizing their struggle and prioritizing their care above all else.

Conclusion: Advocating for Change in India's Healthcare

The corruption and exploitation witnessed in India's healthcare system, especially during COVID-19, have left a lasting impact. But we can work toward a future where healthcare is equitable and humane. This requires consistent pressure on regulatory bodies, policy changes, and a collective effort from the public. Hospitals must be reminded that their role is to serve, not exploit.

By pushing for accountability and transparent practices, we can transform healthcare into a system that values life over money, compassion over profit. Every patient deserves to be treated with dignity, and every family deserves a healthcare experience that respects their humanity.

Additional FAQs

1. **What are the most common ways hospitals exploit patients?**: Hospitals often overcharge for ICU beds, oxygen, and medications, inflate bills with unnecessary tests, and impose hidden fees on patients during emergencies.

2. **How can I avoid being overcharged at a hospital?**: Ask for a detailed bill, question any unfamiliar charges, and compare treatment costs with other hospitals if possible. You may also report excessive charges to regulatory bodies.

3. **Are there patient rights laws in India that can protect me?**: Yes, the Patient Rights Charter includes the right to receive information on costs, consent before procedures, and fair treatment. However, enforcement remains a challenge.

4. **Is health insurance enough to cover exorbitant hospital costs?**: Health insurance can help but may not cover all costs due to policy limitations, and hospitals sometimes inflate bills beyond insurance limits.

5. **What should I do if I face corruption at a hospital?**: Document all details, keep copies of bills, and report the incident to hospital management or a regulatory body like the Medical Council of India. Social media can also amplify your case for greater impact.

6. By becoming informed and advocating for these changes, we can pave the way for a healthcare system that serves the people, not just the profits.

Chapter-17

My Dream to see INDIA A Corruption-Free Nation-Is this Beyond Imagination?

Let's Pledge together to build a corruption-free Nation

Come forward don't think of Complication,

Let the country to achieve its Goal

Listen to your inner voice which is coming right from your Soul,

Follow your heart it gives you the Instruction

Believe me, it will take you in a right Direction,

For any contribution make yourself Eligible

If you stay on your path, you will be called a perfect Tangible,

At last, your contribution will be Counted

History will be written how you Mounted,

Climbing onto the mountain has never been an easy Task

You can do it by removing your evil Mask,

Think of the country think of its Future

It's time to make a century, Let ourselves to Nurture

This poem is written by me is a call to action—a heartfelt appeal for each of us to join hands in building a corruption-free nation. It speaks with a voice that goes beyond words, resonating with a sense of responsibility and pride. The message is clear: true change begins within. By listening to our inner conscience, we are guided to make ethical choices that serve not just ourselves but the greater good.

The poem urges us not to fear the obstacles or complications that stand in the way of progress. It reassures us that if we stay committed to the cause, following our hearts and aligning our actions with the integrity of our souls, we will play an invaluable part in shaping history. Our contributions, though they may seem small, add up to a powerful force that drives our nation forward.

Through vivid imagery, it likens this journey to climbing a mountain—a task that's undeniably challenging. The "evil mask" represents the dishonesty and corruption that need to be stripped away for genuine progress. With an unyielding determination, each one of us has the potential to scale this mountain, to build a future where integrity and justice flourish.

As the poem draws to a close, it reminds us to think of the country's future, to dream big, and to nurture these dreams by committing to the highest ethical standards. It's a collective pledge—a reminder that the nation's destiny is shaped by the honesty and dedication of its people. This is not just poetry; it's a mission, an oath, and a shared dream for a brighter tomorrow.

India, our incredible homeland, is blessed with a rich cultural heritage, abundant natural resources, and a population bursting with energy, talent, and potential. From the Himalayas to the southern tip of Kanyakumari, India stands as a symbol of diversity and unity, resilience, and progress. Yet, a dark shadow looms over this potential—a shadow called corruption. It seeps into almost every part of our daily lives, affecting the aspirations and dreams of millions of honest citizens.

Imagine an India where every rupee of taxpayer money is used for the nation's growth, where there is no need to pay "extra" to get things done, and where honesty is respected more than money. Imagine a country where young minds grow up believing in fairness and justice, and where the rights and opportunities we hold dear are accessible to everyone, regardless of wealth or power. This is the India of my dreams—an India free from the chains of corruption.

Some may say this vision is impossible, that corruption is too deeply rooted in our systems, our institutions, and even our thinking. They argue that corruption is just a part of "how things work" here, that it has become so entrenched it can never be eradicated. But I ask: is it truly beyond our imagination to break free from these chains? I don't think so. I believe that change is possible, and I believe we can make this dream of a corruption-free India a reality.

The Daily Struggles of Corruption

For the average Indian, corruption isn't just a word; it's an everyday reality. It's the reason why a mother stands helplessly outside a government hospital, desperately waiting for treatment for her sick child because she cannot afford to "pay extra" to see the doctor faster. It's why a young man, full of dreams and ready to serve, is forced to pay a bribe to secure a job he deserves by merit alone. It's why hardworking farmers, who pour their sweat and soul into feeding the nation, often fall into debt because middlemen and officials siphon off the support meant for them. Corruption doesn't just steal money—it steals hope, dignity, and the right to a fair life.

Even in small, everyday actions, many Indians encounter corruption. Standing in line to get a driver's license, applying for a government scholarship, trying to secure a place in a good school for a child—all of these can be tainted by the need to offer a bribe or pull strings. It creates an environment where only those who can pay or influence get what they need, while honest citizens suffer. This reality drives a wedge between the people and the systems meant to serve them, breeding a sense of helplessness and resentment.

The Cycle of Corruption

Corruption is a vicious cycle, feeding on itself to create a culture of mistrust and injustice. Once someone gives in to corruption, they often find themselves trapped, unable to escape it. People who pay bribes or work within a corrupt system become part of it, knowingly or unknowingly. Even well-meaning officials or businesspeople are pressured to join this system to survive or advance. They see that refusing to participate in corruption often leads to slower processes, missed opportunities, or even outright retribution. The whole system becomes a web, entangling good people along with the bad.

Sadly, this cycle also teaches the next generation that corruption is "normal" or "necessary." Young people, the future of our nation, see these practices and learn from them. They grow up observing how corruption becomes the shortcut to success, the "way things work." This cycle then strengthens its hold on society, pushing honesty and integrity into the shadows, and making corruption seem like an unbreakable tradition.

Breaking the Chains

But here's the truth: we don't have to accept this reality. Real change begins with awareness and the courage to confront what seems impossible. As citizens, we have immense power in our unity. Our voices, our actions, and our refusal to submit to corrupt practices can be a force too strong for any dishonest system to withstand. If we commit, as a people, to holding our leaders, officials, and even each other accountable, we can spark change that future generations will benefit from.

Imagine if, instead of accepting a demand for a bribe, we demand fair and transparent processes. Imagine if we begin to celebrate and reward honesty, encouraging young people to choose integrity over shortcuts. Imagine a government that not only speaks against corruption but actively works to remove it, punishing those who betray public trust and honoring those who work with integrity.

The Role of Every Citizen

Each one of us has a role to play. Yes, the task is enormous, and it often feels overwhelming. But meaningful change never comes easily. It starts with individuals who are determined to make a difference—people who refuse to participate in corruption, who report dishonest practices, and who encourage others to stand firm. Each honest action is a small victory, a step towards the larger goal of a corruption-free India.

Imagine a nation where every citizen believes in the power of honesty. Imagine children growing up in a world where they see their parents, teachers, and leaders setting examples of integrity. If every Indian decides to make small changes in their daily lives, to resist corruption and advocate for transparency, we can build a movement powerful enough to shake the very foundation of corrupt systems.

A Dream Worth Fighting For

A corruption-free India may seem like a dream, but it's a dream worth fighting for. This vision is not beyond imagination; it's within our reach, as long as we believe in it and work toward it. India has overcome monumental challenges before, from colonial rule to poverty to social inequalities. Corruption is just one more battle on the path to building a stronger, fairer India.

In this book, we will explore not only the issues but also the solutions. We will see examples of countries that have reduced corruption, leaders who stood up against the odds, and citizens who refused to be silenced. Together, we will ignite the courage to dream, to act, and to create a future where honesty prevails, where fairness is the norm, and where every Indian can hold their head high, proud of a corruption-free nation.

A Dream Worth Fighting For

A corruption-free India may seem like a dream, but it's a dream worth fighting for. This vision is not beyond imagination; it's within our reach, as long as we believe in it and work toward it. India has overcome monumental challenges before, from colonial rule to poverty to social inequalities. Corruption is just one more battle on the path to building a stronger, fairer India.

In this book, we will explore not only the issues but also the solutions. We will see examples of countries that have reduced corruption, leaders who stood up against the odds, and citizens who refused to be silenced. Together, we will ignite the courage to dream, to act, and to create a future where honesty prevails, where fairness is the norm, and where every Indian can hold their head high, proud of a corruption-free nation.

A Call for Accountability

For India to become a corruption-free nation, we need strong systems of accountability. This isn't just about setting laws or creating new policies; it's about enforcing them fairly and transparently. Accountability means that every official, regardless of position or power, is answerable to the people. A strong, independent judiciary, an empowered anti-corruption agency, and mechanisms for public oversight are critical for real change.

Imagine if every government office was required to publicly display the steps, costs, and estimated time required for each service it offers. Imagine if citizens had access to channels where they could report bribes or unfair practices without fear of retaliation. These systems are not impossible to create—some countries and states have already implemented similar practices, proving that such measures can work when there's a genuine commitment to rooting out corruption.

Learning from Success Stories

There are countries and regions around the world that have successfully curbed corruption, transforming themselves in the process. Singapore, once plagued by corruption, implemented strict anti-corruption laws, transparent procedures, and severe penalties for offenders. Over time, these efforts built a culture of honesty and integrity, inspiring citizens and government officials alike to take pride in their work and country.

India can learn from these success stories. While our challenges are unique, the fundamental principles are the same: accountability, transparency, and fair enforcement. These are the building blocks of an honest society, and they require a united effort from every sector of society—government, businesses, and citizens alike.

The Role of Technology

Technology offers us powerful tools to combat corruption. Digital systems for tracking payments, online platforms for government services, and open databases that allow citizens to monitor projects and spending can all help increase transparency. With a smartphone in almost every hand and internet access steadily increasing, India is in a unique position to leverage technology to fight corruption.

E-governance initiatives, like online portals for property registration, driver's license applications, and tax payments, reduce the need for face-to-face interactions where corruption often occurs. Digital transactions leave an electronic trail, making it harder for corrupt practices to go unnoticed. Technology can also empower citizens to report corruption instantly and anonymously, building a network of people committed to honesty and fairness.

Empowering Education and Youth

Education is another critical weapon against corruption. Imagine if every young Indian grew up learning not only about academic subjects but also about ethics, civic responsibility, and the true cost of corruption. Teaching children the value of honesty, respect for laws, and the power of integrity can shape the next generation of citizens who will uphold these values naturally.

India is blessed with a large youth population, full of potential and a hunger for change. The energy and ideals of young Indians are our greatest asset in this fight. When young people stand up for justice, they inspire others, challenging old norms and daring to create a better future. Youth-led initiatives, from anti-corruption rallies to social media campaigns, can create ripples across the nation, spreading awareness and encouraging everyone to say no to corruption.

Small Steps with Big Impact

Sometimes, the enormity of corruption makes it feel insurmountable. But change doesn't have to start with grand gestures; even small steps taken by individuals can have a significant impact. Here are a few everyday actions each of us can take to contribute to a corruption-free India:

1. **Refuse to Pay Bribes** – This may be difficult, and it may mean waiting longer or facing obstacles, but refusing to pay a bribe is a powerful way to resist corruption. When more people refuse, corrupt officials will have fewer opportunities to demand illicit payments.

2. **Report Corruption** – Many organizations and platforms allow citizens to report corrupt practices anonymously. Using these channels ensures that wrongdoings are exposed and encourages others to follow suit.

3. **Educate and Encourage** – Talk to friends, family, and community members about the negative effects of corruption. Encourage those around you to make honest choices and to resist the urge to take or offer shortcuts through dishonest means.

4. **Participate in Civic Life** – Voting, attending public hearings, and joining community organizations give citizens a voice. When people are involved in local governance, they can demand transparency and accountability from their leaders.

5. **Support Transparent Businesses** – Many businesses are committed to ethical practices. By supporting companies that prioritize integrity, consumers can help promote a market where honesty is valued.

The Power of Collective Action

Corruption cannot survive in a society that refuses to tolerate it. Collective action—the power of ordinary people coming together for a common cause—is one of the most effective ways to bring about change. When citizens unite, they form a force that can stand up to even the most powerful individuals or institutions.

In India, we've seen how citizens, when united, can challenge deeply entrenched issues. Our independence movement, our fight for rights, and our response to natural disasters all show how Indians can come together to tackle big problems. If we channel that same spirit toward eradicating corruption, there's no doubt we can succeed.

A Brighter Tomorrow

Imagine an India where every child is given an equal chance, every worker is rewarded fairly, and every official serves with integrity. This is the India of our dreams, an India that reflects the values of honesty, fairness, and pride in one's work. The road to this vision may be long and challenging, but with every step we take, we come closer to making it a reality.

In this journey, every Indian has a role to play. Together, we can create a future where integrity is celebrated, corruption is rejected, and every citizen has a reason to believe in their country. Let us commit to this vision with courage, resilience, and unwavering hope.